GENIOCRACY

"Nothing in the universe can resist a sufficiently large number of linked and organized intellects."

Teilhard de Chardin

GENIOCRACY

*Government of the People,
for the People, by the Geniuses*

RAEL

Translated from the French "La Geniocratie" by Rael, originally published in 1977 by "La Fondation Raëlienne".

First English Edition

ISBN-10: 2-940252-19-X
ISBN-13: 978-2-940252-19-0

Publisher: Nova Distribution
The publisher may be contacted at: publisher@rael.org

Credits:
Chief Editor and Project Manager: Cameron Hanly
Composition and Design: Cameron Hanly and Rob Chalfant
Cover Art: Julian Winfield and Cameron Hanly
Translation: Marcus Wenner and Eva Ponty
Proofreading: Kathy Watterson

CONTENTS

CHARTS

Preface by Marcel Terrusse

Chemical Engineer

I trembled with enthusiasm while reading this book.

We're all apprehensive about the future of humanity, but "Geniocracy" reduces our apprehension by showing us that solutions to the political, economic, and social problems we're facing do exist. It helps us realize that our planet's management and organization require choices at a level of responsibility much too important to be handled by traditional politicians.

In fact, we're at a crossroads. We've dedicated much effort to the development of a technological society. Nevertheless, we've kept habits inherited from the past, and our social and political structures are becoming more and more outdated.

We need to recognize that our planet is a global village, and that the fates of all human beings are interconnected. Our survival depends on this consciousness, and it also depends on individual efforts to develop the tolerance and love that suppress aggressiveness and calm the passions.

To avoid the dangers inherent in our aggressive tendencies, reason must take over.

It's nonsense to pass judgment on science, for knowledge is desirable. It's the interpretation given to applications derived from that knowledge – by political decisions or private interests – that causes the public to either welcome beneficial discoveries or shun them for fear of possible evil applications.

This is a problem of politics and societal choice, but it is also one of generosity and altruism. By becoming aware of our blindness and lack of realism, we can change our society. Lucidity, courage, pragmatism and intelligence will allow us to enter a Golden Age governed by genius.

I'm profoundly impressed by this book's proposals for selective democracy and by the project of establishing a geniocratic society. I enthusiastically support these ideas. In fact, I was amazed by the clarity of the reasoning and the simplicity of the ideas. Starting with the observation of our present foolish ways, the author ends up proposing a radical transformation of our habits and society.

This book was born from the meditations of a man of superior intelligence and is the result of an extraordinary work of synthesis done with the greatest lucidity. It was guided by a profound love for human beings, and by the concern to preserve their real interests – not the material interests of a minority that subsists through self-protection, isolating itself behind borders and the walls of its safes.

Is it acceptable that those in power today wield that power only because a confused and manipulated population is unable to make lucid choices?

This book will upset a few people, but what does that matter compared to the collective interest and the very future of humanity?

Giving concrete expression to the proposals in this book will require a huge effort from all of us, but what joy we'll know when we do! We'll have the serenity of living in confidence in a society based on the only true values: those attached to the individual and his intelligence.

We are the masters of our destiny, and it's up to us to either enter a Golden Age governed by reason or allow lethargy and fear of change to halt humanity's thousands of years of progress.

We alone are responsible. It's up to us to understand, and it's up to us to act. "Geniocracy" by Rael shows us how. It is a book of love, genius and hope.

PREFACE BY MICHEL DEYDIER

Psychologist

Of all the qualities, intelligence contains the purest and most useful energy.

It is through his brain and its acts of intelligence that man organizes his vital center, and when he decides to enter a group, that vital center expands dramatically and its organization needs to be modified to prevent failure.

Great minds have always acknowledged this psychological foundation. It would be insane to deny psychobiological realities within sociology, or to deny the inequality of human and animal brain structures. We must acknowledge the existence of a hierarchy in levels of consciousness, of reflection.

It's encouraging to note that irrationality and nonsense are progressively disappearing from neuro-psychological laboratories, where knowledge of biostructural organization started to emerge a few years ago. Such an opportunity shouldn't be missed, for scientific knowledge isn't an occult cookbook – or at least it shouldn't be anymore.

In this book, Rael has remarkably analyzed and synthesized the fundamental ideas of our civilization.

Issues related to individual psychological fulfillment are addressed in a very sound manner, and the principles and social plans of action described match psychobiological needs with unprecedented accuracy. A specialist's eye will notice with interest the proposal to establish awakening centers, where everyone could reach mental fulfillment through techniques that awaken creativity and release tensions and mental blocks, and where our children could experience what we've missed in the legitimate development of inner potential, abilities and tastes according to personality.

However, such fulfillment isn't the only advantage we can expect. Through psychological testing of children, teenagers and adults, we can detect negative tendencies – including inhibitions, self-destructiveness, and propensities toward violence, criminality and sadism. Sophisticated detection on a larger scale could prevent crime before completely finding a cure for it, thus eliminating most offences and acts of violence.

But it's not my intent to elaborate on the treasures this book contains. We all have the ability to think for ourselves. Those who do will recognize in the following pages the humanistic purpose of the World Geniocratic Movement, which consists of science, genius and love.

INTRODUCTION

This book is addressed to everyone who wishes that the World War of 1939-1945 be truly the last, and that the atomic bomb used at Hiroshima be the last used to kill innocent people. It is also addressed to scientists, geniuses and inventors who can no longer bear to see their discoveries exploited by political and military powers for murderous ends; and to people who are neither scientists nor geniuses nor inventors, but nevertheless believe that those best able to pull this world out of the fetid mess it's in, languishing under the permanent threat of total destruction, are those with the most imagination and ability to invent new paradigms and world structures adapted to our present civilization – in other words, the scientists, geniuses and inventors.

To govern is to foresee. Those now governing us have foreseen nothing; therefore they are not capable of governing.

And why are those governing us so incompetent?

They're incompetent because they were elected for their job democratically. Pure democracy cannot take voter intelligence into account, which means the voice of an Einstein is given no greater weight than that of an idiot. And since there are far more idiots than Einsteins, we find ourselves under the dictatorship of idiocy. We need only look around us to see the consequences of living under such a dictatorship.

Crude democracy cannot avoid being a "mediocracy", since

those with mediocre intelligence are by definition the majority. ("Mediocre" comes from the Latin *medius*, or "middle.")

Geniocracy, on the other hand, uses selective democracy to place in power those whose intelligence is above average, rather than just appoint those who attended prestigious schools, as we do now. Geniuses can be found just as frequently among the working or peasant class as among the educated. It is these natural geniuses who should take the destiny of humanity in hand before it is too late.

Isn't it the most natural of things to wish that the world be governed by people of above-average intelligence?

There have always been doomsday prophets announcing the end of the world, but they had no scientific evidence with which to frighten the population. However, these "millennium prophets" are now eminent scientists, atheist philosophers and even heads of states, because for the first time in human history, man has the means to destroy all life on his own planet, to self-destruct in a grand nuclear cataclysm.

This possibility has never occurred before in all the thousands of years man has existed on Earth, and we have the privilege – yes, I say the privilege – to live in this epoch. We have the privilege to be responsible for either the extinction of our species or its entry into the Golden Age, into a new civilization based on love, fraternity and fulfillment.

You who are about to read these next few lines are one of those responsible for this ultimate choice, and you will answer to all future generations yet to come – or not to come. Don't read these lines as an idle spectator, but as an actor, because this concerns you. It is your life – or your death!

I. PRINCIPLES OF GENIOCRACY

A Short History of Government Types

"The republic does not need scientists."
(pronounced at Lavoisier's trial)

"All men are stupid without science."

THE HOLY BIBLE - JEREMIAH X

How has mankind governed itself from the very beginning?

First, the strongest physically imposed their will on others.

Thanks to their physical strength, they accumulated goods and riches.

Their children inherited those riches, so rule by the strong was replaced with rule by the rich.

As these possessors of riches governed, they took care to acquire the knowledge gained through discoveries made by their most intelligent subjects.

They then made sure that not everyone got hold of this knowledge, so as to establish a government of people possessing knowledge.

These possessors of knowledge deemed themselves inherently superior and thereby exploited, oppressed, and mistreated their people.

The people finally overthrew the knowledge possessors and democratically elected knowledge possessors to govern them.

This meant: *knowledge in power.*

But knowledge is not intelligence, and that is the problem.

3

Knowledge is no more than simple acts of memorization that any old computer can do. In itself, it certainly cannot solve any problems.

So the knowledge possessors used the inventions provided by well-intentioned geniuses for their own murderous ends, exploiting them to affirm their own power.

The government composed of knowledge possessors then established top-level schools to teach how to administrate and govern by using and exploiting other people's inventions.

We must replace leadership by knowledge with leadership by genius. None of our great academic institutions creates geniuses; they produce only well-polished memories. Common sense and intelligence have nothing to do with whether one has been to school or not.

Every generation has had inventors who were used each time by those in power to put humanity in danger. And each time, these betrayed and exploited inventors grieved when they saw their inventions used to kill innocent people.

This cannot continue!

It's time to put in power those who make – and have always made – humanity progress. They are neither muscle-bound brutes, nor hoarders of riches, nor possessors of knowledge, nor politicians, nor soldiers. These others have all had their turn to govern and show what they were capable of doing when they ruled the world. It is only the geniuses who have never been given a chance to show what they can do as rulers!

Had Einstein known how his invention was to be used, he would never have allowed it. When he did realize, it was too late: The organized brutes of the military were already flying their fortresses toward Hiroshima.

Geniuses must unite and ensure sole control over use of their inventions. They must resist political and military pressure and assert their independence and desire for non-violence.

It is long overdue for mankind to benefit from its most important asset: geniuses.

HOW THE TYPES OF GOVERNMENT EVOLVE

Type of government	Government founded on:	Characterized by:
Brutes	Force	Muscular strength
Possessors	Inherited riches accumulated by brutes, allowing them to hire muscle for commanding respect.	Riches
Possessors	Jealously guarded knowledge and continued protection thanks to hired muscle.	Riches
Knowers	Elected (by the people) after possessors who oppressed the people are overthrown.	Knowledge, plus riches that allow them to control propaganda.
Military	Use of knowledge devoted to organized violence.	Use of arms, plus the brainwashing of young men (conditioning them to obey any order.)
Geniuses	Intelligence	Common sense, imagination, ability to link things together. In a word: genius.

How to Place Geniuses in Power

"Intelligent people will shine like the light on the firmament and those who brought justice like the stars."

The Holy Bible, Daniel Xii

Humanity can be compared to a human body, each cell of which corresponds to an individual. Some cells are made to be part of an organ that serves the whole to move or digest food, etc., and some are made to be part of the place in charge of making decisions – of choosing the direction in which the body will walk, what food it will absorb, etc; this place is the brain. The cells of the brain are the most capable of doing these tasks, which is why they're located in this organ – not because the other cells placed them there after an election.

Unfortunately, that is not the case for humanity, for some cells designed to be in the foot find themselves in the brain, which explains all the problems we have today.

Brain cells aren't superior to foot cells. Instead, they're complementary, for without the foot, the brain wouldn't be able to move, and therefore couldn't survive; and without the brain, the foot wouldn't know which direction to move in, so it wouldn't survive either.

Therefore, it's imperative that those more able than others to think, reflect, and imagine be used to direct society – just as the human body uses the cells of the brain in that way.

Putting geniuses at the service of humanity: This is what geniocracy is all about.

CRUDE DEMOCRACY: MEDIOCRACY

"It is not because no one sees the truth that it becomes a mistake."

GANDHI

What we presently call democracy is in fact mediocracy, since people of average intelligence are more numerous. Therefore, it is *their* decisions that prevail in elections.

Following extremely sophisticated tests, one can see by looking at the resulting bell curve for intelligence that the super-gifted and geniuses - who constitute only the top 0.5 percent of the population – have their votes cancelled out by the mentally retarded, the bottom 0.5 percent!

The gifted make up only 2 percent of the population, and their voices are cancelled out by the mentally backward, who also make up 2 percent!

Votes of those whose intelligence is 10 to 30 percent above average – the "above average" who constitute 25 percent of the population – are cancelled out by those whose intelligence is 10 to 30 percent below average, who also constitute 25 percent of the population.

That leaves the remaining 45 percent to cast ballots. They have an average, and therefore mediocre, intelligence (mediocre comes from the Latin *medios*, or average). That's why this form of democracy is, in fact, a mediocracy.

9

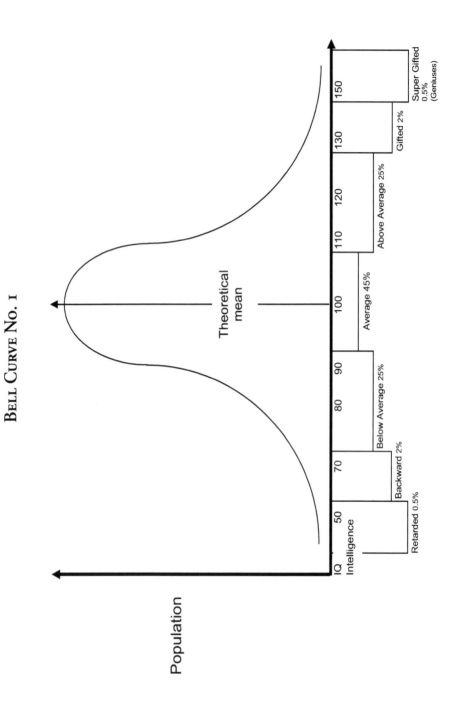

GENIOCRACY: SELECTIVE DEMOCRACY

*"Those who never admit they were wrong love
themselves more than the truth."*

J. JOUBERT

The basic principle of geniocracy consists of measuring the raw intelligence (which has nothing to do with the number of diplomas someone has) of the entire population by using sophisticated scientific tests. This done, only those whose raw intelligence is more than 10 percent above the average would be given the right to vote, and only those whose intelligence is more than 50 percent above the average (the geniuses) would be eligible to govern.

What is more natural than wishing that those governing indeed be the most intelligent?

But it's essential that the intelligence tests in no way favor those from top academic institutions, or those with numerous diplomas. The tests must be applied to laborers, peasants and engineers in a balanced, unbiased way. Then geniuses will be drawn from all social classes, all races and both sexes, and the process will therefore be truly democratic. It will be a *selective* democracy.

As shown on the geniocratic bell curve, this system ensures that the voices of geniuses, the gifted and the above average aren't cancelled out by the retarded, the backward and the below average. Therefore, only 27.5 percent of the population will have a voice during elections.

It must be stressed that the mere fact of being a genius doesn't automatically carry with it the right to be part of the government. It only bestows the right to be a candidate. It is from the pool of geniuses that the more intelligent members of the population will democratically elect those they think most capable of forming a government.

Therefore, a geniocracy is a democratic system of government.

Geniocracy and Fascism

Many talk about fascism, but few really know what it means. Let's consult a dictionary. *Fascism*: dictatorship of a single party.

A geniocracy therefore can't be considered a fascist system, since geniuses from both the right and the left – with a wide range of viewpoints – can be part of the government and represent parties of all types. In contrast, a fascist government is composed solely of members who belong to and represent the viewpoint of a sole legal party that prohibits the existence of other parties.

In fact, one could say that the systems in place today in China, Chile and Russia – and other such countries where only one party is legally authorized – are fascist.

Geniocracy is a system of government, not a political party. It accepts all political viewpoints within the context of its governmental system.

Bell Curve No. 2

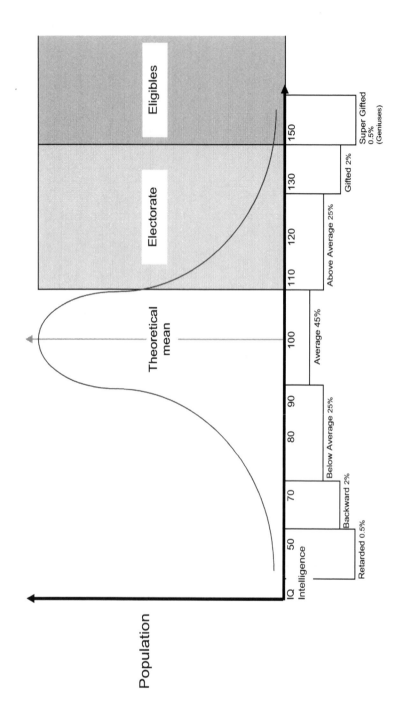

GENIOCRACY, ELITISM AND ARISTOCRACY

"Man fears nothing on Earth more than reason;
he fears it more than ruin and even death."

BERTRAND RUSSELL

These days, it's almost fashionable to treat intelligence as a shameful disease. Faced with the terrible injustices that existed in the past – some of which we still haven't eradicated – humanity has quite rightly tried to create a more egalitarian society. While we can certainly congratulate ourselves on our wish to ensure that all people benefit from equal opportunities and are able to fulfill themselves completely, we must take a stand when, under the pretext of total and absolute equality, no more attention is given to the opinion of a genius than to that of someone mentally retarded. Yet this is what crude democracy does.

Equal opportunity to all for fulfillment in life is essential, but without taking level of intelligence into account, equality of opinions for making important decisions is nonsense.

Humans must be given equal rights from birth, yet are born with different abilities. Since everyone is born different, why try to make everyone the same? Certainly the environment plays an important role in individual fulfillment, but given equal nurturing, a genius remains a genius and someone born mentally subnormal remains subnormal.

15

All children must have equal opportunity to mature in an environment best suited for developing their individual talents, and their education must be adapted to allow geniuses and gifted individuals to emerge. But this process must not exclude giving appreciation to the rarest gems: the geniuses.

The frightening image of the mad genius who wants to rule the world and blow up the planet is often used to discredit intelligence in the eyes of the population. That way, nobody notices that our present governments want to do just that. They want to dominate the world and accumulate weapons capable of destroying the planet, and this is true precisely because these governments are not made up of geniuses themselves.

Note that geniocracy is not dictatorship by one man, but the creation of a world college of many hundreds of geniuses from all corners of the earth. We benefit daily from the fruits of the imagination, thoughts and work of geniuses. Throughout the day, we use objects invented thanks to the brains of people with above-average intelligence. From the light bulb to the television, the bicycle to the motorcar, the cold-water tap to the washing machine, the typewriter to the tape recorder, the piano to the hi-fi; all these objects that make our lives more comfortable and easier are here thanks to people able to find new solutions to problems by using their intelligence.

Any mentally retarded person commonly uses one or several of these objects without being capable of understanding how they function. Nevertheless, his or her life improves through using them.

All this is quite natural. Geniocracy aims to transpose what is true at the level of objects and apply it at the level of government, allowing the gifted to benefit the less gifted. That is geniocracy.

If we had voted democratically to decide whether some inventions

16

should be used or not, almost all of them would have been rejected, and we would still be travelling on horses and carts in the streets of Paris. The automobile, the airplane and the railroad were all strongly criticized at the time of their invention, and if they had been put to the public vote, they surely would have been prohibited. Only geniuses, whose imaginations allow them to foresee further than others, are able to understand the immense possibilities of their discoveries.

The same is true today for computers, the atom and genetic research.

How can we realistically expect people incapable of imagining what tomorrow's world will be like to make decisions in preparation for the future?

To govern is to foresee. Therefore, we must place in government those able to foresee and understand the consequences of their actions, even if the majority of humanity can't fully understand why certain precautions are taken.

If you had gangrene infecting your hand, you would have to cut it off to prevent the infection from spreading to the rest of your body and eventually killing you. The other hand or leg can't make such a decision. Only the brain can foresee what might happen in the future, so it gives the order to get rid of the infected member before it's too late.

Today we prefer mediocrity to quality, and words such as *elitism*, *aristocracy* and *nobility* have become taboo. But that's because they have now come to symbolize something different from their original meaning.

It's useful to understand the real meanings of these words. Once again, let's consult the dictionary. *Elite:* that which is best or most distinguished.

Geniocracy seeks to place the most intelligent – the geniuses – in power, and such geniuses have what is best in terms of imagination. Therefore, we can say that a geniocratic system is an elitist system.

It's surprising to see that those who say elitism is abominable suddenly forget their principles and do all they can to get their sick children to the "best" doctors and the "best" surgeons. And of course that is quite natural.

The word *elite* has long been used to describe a financially privileged social class, which because of its wealth was able to acquire an above-average level of knowledge. But those elite don't interest us. It's the elite of intelligence – not of money or knowledge – who will ensure a geniocratic government.

It's the same for the word *aristocracy*.

Again, let's look it up in the dictionary. *Aristocracy*: government exercised by the nobility (from the Greek: *aristos*, excellent; and *kratos*, power).

So aristocracy means power of the excellent.

Let's check the dictionary. *Excellent*: superior in its genre, perfect.

Geniocracy aims to give power to those possessing an excellent ("superior, perfect") intelligence. So we can also say a geniocratic system is an aristocracy – but once again, an aristocracy not of money or knowledge, but of intelligence.

The dictionary adds that an aristocracy is "a government exercised by the noble class". Let's look up the definition of this word. *Noble*: illustrious, of resplendent merit (from the Latin, *nobilis*).

Geniocracy aims to put those having the merit of above-average intelligence in power. Therefore, we could say geniocracy is a true form of aristocracy because it seeks to place the fully noble in power, but here we're talking about nobility of mind – not nobility of financial wealth or that defined by title.

Finally, there is one more word whose original meaning is worth looking up, and that is the word "monarchy". *Monarchy*: a regime directed by a chief of state, elected or hereditary, in whom resides political authority.

Therefore, we could say that our familiar presidential systems, put in place democratically, are actually monarchies, for even the most serious decisions concerning nuclear war, right of pardon, etc., depend on just one man. In contrast, geniocracy ensures that no decision can ever depend on just one man. Instead, decisions are made by a college of geniuses.

Elitism, *aristocracy*, *nobility* and *monarchy:* These are words whose original meanings are important to retrace.

ESTABLISHING GENIOCRACY

"There will be no end to human problems so long as philosophers are not kings and kings are not philosophers."

SOCRATES

The first step in setting up a geniocratic system is to establish who among the population will have the right to vote (the electors) and who will be eligible to stand for election (the eligibles). The former will be those whose level of basic intelligence is more than 10 percent above the average, while the latter will be those whose level is more than 50 percent above it.

Therefore, we must first select the means that enables us to define each person's level of intelligence. In other words, we must ask specialists – psychologists, neurologists, ethnologists, etc. – to perfect or choose from existing tests those that allow us to achieve this goal.

The tests must be designed in such a way that they don't disadvantage any level of society. They must give everyone an equal chance, whether literate or not, educated or not, laborers or engineers, peasants or academics. Once again, let's not forget that the goal is to measure basic intelligence, not education or culture. In other words, the goal is good old common sense, not whether someone has spent many years accumulating knowledge. It is *practical* intelligence that we wish to measure.

Before going any further, we must define what we mean by intelligence. According to G. Viaud:

> "All acts of intelligence are characterized by an understanding of the relationships between the given elements of a situation and the invention of what needs to be done using those elements to solve the problem and achieve the goal."

This definition is one of those that best corresponds to the type of intelligence we're interested in, and it confirms what the majority of psychologists propose: *Intelligence is the capacity to use given information in a way relevant to a particular situation.*

That's why it's so important for the tests to use information understandable to all, of every culture and background. Therefore, using these tests, we'll be able to measure each person's intelligence, and define it not according to I.Q. (intellectual quotient) but according to I.P. (intellectual potential). This determination mustn't take age into account either. Whatever the age, we're interested only in intelligence.

The fact that we presently give the vote to an idiot just because he is 18 years old, yet exclude a 16-year-old genius only because he or she is under the voting age, is proof of how maladapted our present crude democracy is.

Once the intelligence of the entire population has been established, it will be easy to calculate the mean, and to give voting rights only to those whose level of intelligence is more than 10 percent above that mean, and the right to stand for elections only to those more than 50 percent above the mean (the geniuses). The electors can then elect their government from the pool of eligibles – the geniuses – in the most truly democratic way possible.

To give an idea of the proportions for a country such as France: Instead of having 30 million electors – as we had in 1977, for example – allowing only those whose intelligence is more than 10 percent above average to vote would have resulted in an electorate of 27.5 percent of 30 million, or 8,250,000 people, who would have elected their government from the pool of geniuses (those with intelligence more than 50 percent above the average) who made up only 0.5 percent of the population but numbered 150,000 nonetheless.

Isn't it encouraging to realize there are 150,000 geniuses in France? Isn't it high time we took account of their opinions?

And if we were to think in terms of world population, we would get 660 million electors and 20 million eligibles for office: 20 million geniuses to save four billion human beings, on the condition that we allow them to take things in hand.

The tests would need to be taken by the entire population every seven years so that individual development could be taken into account. Some geniuses remain blocked by personality problems and only reveal themselves after overcoming these psychological inhibitions.

At each test cycle, the average will certainly vary, most probably increasing each time as the standard of living rises, as scientific discoveries liberate humanity, and as the population fulfills itself more and more. So it might turn out that someone measured as a genius today could simply be an elector tomorrow if the average level of intelligence catches up with him.

Teenagers could take the test as soon as they become sufficiently mature, and from then on every seven years along with everyone else.

Some people who don't qualify as electors at age 18 because they're not among those more than 10 percent above average might very possibly enter that category seven years later, after resolving certain psychological inhibitions.

By the same token, some people able to be electors at age 74 might lose this right seven years later, at 81, if their intellectual faculties have suffered from aging.

Isn't it ridiculous to see the number of present-day voters so senile that they have to be carried to the voting station? This is yet another example of how very maladapted crude democracy is!

The same principle would apply to the eligibles: Someone whose level fell to less than 50 percent above average – perhaps due to senility or an accident – would lose eligibility.

ACCESS TO THE REGIONAL COLLEGE OF GENIUSES

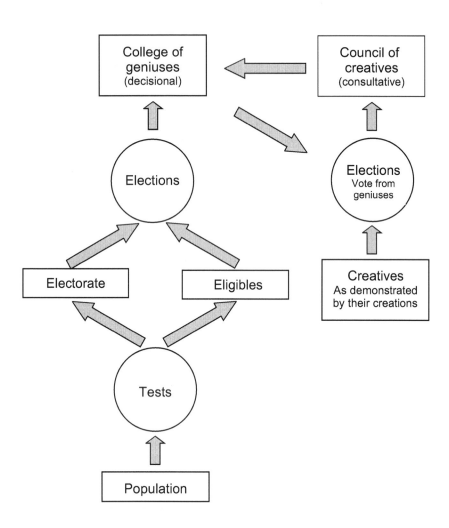

The Basic Aims of Geniocracy

- To make Earth a world of happiness and fulfillment for all inhabitants, without prejudice as to race, religion, culture, or level of intelligence, by establishing a world government composed of people selected from a pool of geniuses by the most intelligent.

- To use all means to achieve this goal.

- To abolish individual and mass violence.

- To replace the right to work with the right to fulfillment.

- To save humanity from destroying itself, the risk of which is largely due to the lack of intelligence in the leaders it has given itself.

Those are the five fundamental goals of geniocracy, which we will now go over point by point.

CREATION OF A WORLD GENIOCRATIC GOVERNMENT

To govern is to foresee. Those governing have foreseen nothing and are thereby incapable of governing.

Therefore, it is a matter of urgency now to create a world government composed of those who can foresee: the geniuses.

Looking back in time, we can see that the kings used the geniuses of their times to ensure long reigns and posterity. Great painters, sculptors, architects and even musicians were paid to praise the sovereigns. They were "state" artists. This is, by the way, a little like what is currently happening in the countries of the East, among others. In fact, we can say it happens everywhere, except that this situation no long applies only to artists. It has been expanded to include the scientists – those who allow nations to envision a supremacy that isn't only cultural.

For example, scientists have no choice if they want do pure research: They must either enter state-run national institutes or resign themselves to routine work in purely commercial organizations.

Obviously, in state institutions, they're not free to do what they want. Instead, they have to follow programs imposed on them – programs almost purely motivated by political-military interests so as to be immediately profitable.

This creates the following paradox: The geniuses must follow the directives of the mediocres!

What geniocracy seeks is to let the geniuses themselves define in which direction they wish to work, and to allow them to give themselves the means to do that.

What marks an epoch? The geniuses. We've all heard of Pierre and Marie Curie and Einstein, but nobody can remember the foolish rulers, whose decisions and mistakes these geniuses had to endure. And it's clear which group – geniuses or rulers – acted to improve living conditions for humanity.

Politicians make promises to obtain advantages for themselves, while geniuses work to improve the lives of everyone. Who deserves to govern?

Isn't it the least to ask for – that people of above-average intelligence govern us?

I don't know if I'm above average in intelligence, but I do know I want to be governed by people I'm certain are more intelligent than I am.

Currently, we know our government's leaders were brought up in a more privileged environment than ours, that they frequented famous schools, and that they have plenty of money and lots of contacts. But these aren't the right criteria for us to choose them as leaders! Erudition and the accumulation of knowledge are of no use whatsoever in the age of pocket computers and information technology.

The human being of tomorrow doesn't need to know a lot, but instead must be able to feel, analyze, synthesize and very quickly choose the computerized information that is necessary for understanding, thereby freeing human beings from the constraints of recall.

In fact, thanks to science – and particularly to information technology – the new human being will be able to return to a childlike purity in which he will only have to know the big principles, allowing him to choose his way and be supplied when he needs by the knowledge stored in the omnipresent machines that exist to serve him.

Instead of having to clutter their brains with detailed data, they will access these details anytime from the numerous machines available, which will liberate them in the sense that, when making decisions, they will need to know only the overall picture.

Make way for pure intelligence!

Since governments don't give geniuses the power they deserve, it's up to them to take it, and on a world scale. How? By creating a Provisional World Geniocratic Government in a neutral country. This government will be composed of scientists who refuse to see the fruits of their research fall into the hands of the military and the politicians. In the longer term, they can plan on setting up a research center, to be paid for initially by those seeking to establish geniocracy. If those concerned agree, the center can be maintained by commercializing products and peaceful inventions of the scientists working there.

In fact, this World Geniocratic Government could embargo the fruits of its thinking and research for the first five years, showing them only to a team of independent observers. In this way, it could prove to the world how, had it really been in power, it could have avoided all the mistakes the present "mediocratic" government made. It would also prevent the mediocratic government from stealing the geniocratic government's ideas and taking all the glory. Highlighting the present mediocratic government's mistakes in this manner will do much to discredit it, and will encourage the people of that country to elect representatives of the Geniocratic Party during the next round of elections.

Thus, through its actions, the World Geniocratic Government will encourage the creation of national movements for geniocracy throughout the world. The goal is not to impose geniocracy, but to establish it democratically by showing the necessity of abandoning crude democracy in favor of the selective democracy of geniocracy.

Obviously, when a country's population democratically elects a national party favoring world geniocracy, the World Geniocratic Government will automatically govern it. And as more countries choose geniocracy, those parties will fill the members' seats in the World Geniocratic Government until at least half of humanity has chosen world geniocracy. The rest will then have to accept the democratic decision, and finally the people of Earth will be united.

All those who contributed to this union will have earned eternal gratitude from humanity.

And this means you. You reading these lines have the chance to be pioneers of intelligence and fraternity. You can decide you're no longer satisfied with simply being spectators of the history of humanity and decide to be actors on this huge stage called Earth. In fact, on this stage, even spectators are actors, whether they like it or not. Even if we're happy as spectators, we're still actors – just actors unaware of playing their parts. Our awareness must begin now.

GENIOCRACY AND COLLEGIALITY

Mention the word "genius" and there is always someone who comes up with the stereotype of the mad genius world dominator, as if intelligence were a dangerous disease. But this stereotype is impossible under a geniocratic system, which ensures that one person alone cannot govern the world. Instead, geniocracy is government by a college of several hundred geniuses.

Such a collegial system ensures that no decision can be made by any single person. In this aspect, it is unlike systems of today in which the president acting alone – unfortunately – has sole decisional control over such matters as granting pardons or starting a nuclear war. In a so-called democratic country today, one brain alone – and not necessarily a particularly brilliant one at that – can decide the fate of a human life, and, more importantly, make decisions about the lives of millions of innocent people, or even about the complete destruction of humanity. This is still more evidence of the stupidity inherent in crude democracy!

Our present presidential regimes, the result of such crude democracy, are becoming uncannily close to the past royalist regimes they were supposed to replace. We could almost say that the president is in a position, with no justification needed, to decide the fate of someone on death row – or to spark a nuclear war – simply because "such is his privilege and pleasure". Just as it was with the sovereigns of old!

But under a collegiate system, such rule is impossible. While there may certainly be a president of the College of Geniuses in the world government, this person will not be able to make any decision alone. At most, he or she will preside over the college's meetings and announce the results of its votes. The presidential position will be primarily honorific, with the president representing the college at official ceremonies, such as inaugurations, etc.

Bear in mind that the College of Geniuses will contain a multitude of opinions from members with different positions and viewpoints. For that reason, it would be good to have the members vote only after expressing their varied and differing opinions, if they so wish. However, rather than shout out those views and attempt to influence each other through verbal contortions of spurious value – as so often happens in many parliamentary situations – the members could express their opinions in writing. That way, each member could judge the content, not the cover.

In fact, anonymity of written opinions would ensure that each genius judges matters solely for himself or herself. Members of the College of Geniuses could thereby focus purely on the merits of decisions rather than be swayed by the author of an opinion or by any leftist or rightist camp.

The vote itself could be made electronically through keyboards, thereby guaranteeing complete confidentiality and preventing the phenomenon of "contagion" that occurs with raised hands. The college members might even decide to sit in isolated booths so votes wouldn't be influenced by neighboring reactions.

Obviously all these measures will be studied by the geniuses themselves, who will certainly find many other ways to improve the system.

Another point, most important to understand, is that geniuses aren't found solely among scientists. Most people associate the word "genius" with the "mad scientist" cliché, but plenty of geniuses are also to be found among philosophers, painters, poets, musicians and peasants. The College of the World Geniocratic Government will therefore include not only scientists but philosophers, painters, poets, musicians and peasants.

Bridging the gap between science and art, between the physical sciences and the social sciences, and between science and consciousness, is what geniocracy is all about.

Most of today's problems are due to stunning advances in technology misused because of an accompanying virtual stagnation in consciousness. Though a basic understanding of science has percolated into the general population, advanced consciousness is still the attainment of but a handful of philosophers. Thus, we use tomorrow's technology with yesterday's consciousness. Geniocracy will strive to raise consciousness at least to equal par with technology.

In fact, Gordon Rattray Taylor reaches the same conclusion in his great book, "The Biological Revolution." After reviewing all the amazing things science brings us today and will continue to bring in the future, he concludes by saying, "We must all read the books of wisdom."[3]

ACCESS TO THE WORLD GENIOCRATIC COLLEGE

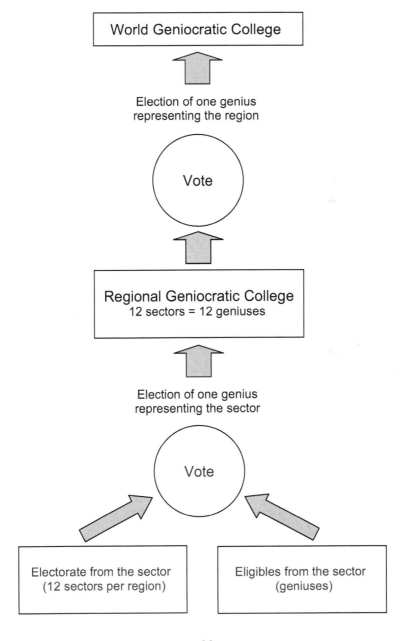

ACCESS TO THE COUNCIL OF CREATIVES

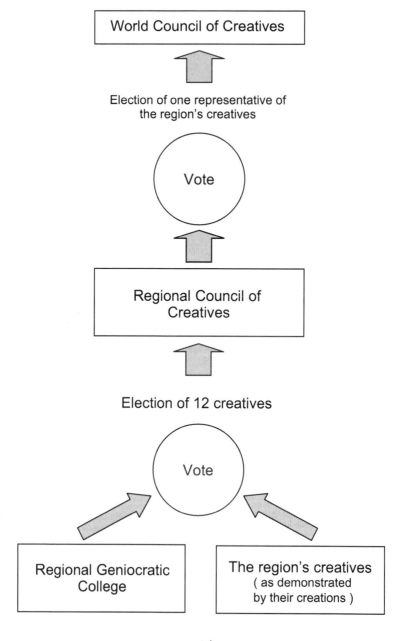

COMPOSITION OF THE
WORLD GENIOCRATIC GOVERNMENT

As we saw earlier, the World Geniocratic Government should be composed of highly intelligent people, but it's important that this type of intelligence be of the practical, methodical, problem-solving kind that is able to make connections. However, there is a type of genius – creative genius – that tests might not be able to detect, even though such individuals represent enormous potential for the progress of humanity. Therefore we must establish a system that allows this type of genius to contribute to the world government.

Creative geniuses can turn up in any field: art, science, philosophy, etc. On the basis of their work, discoveries or creations, names of creative geniuses will be proposed by the regional geniuses. From this pool, a certain number will be elected by the World College of Geniuses to create a Council of Creatives. Although this council will have no decision-making power, it will be able to imagine and propose solutions to problems and suggest projects that could improve the lot of humanity.

These creative solutions and projects will be submitted to the College of Geniuses, which will democratically decide which proposals to apply or pursue.

For a Regional World Geniocracy

The only reasonable way to envision the future of humanity is in global terms.

Throughout the ages, humans were confined to tribes, villages and provinces, and then to states. But faced with problems of pollution and the proliferation of nuclear weapons, intelligent people soon realized that the only way to solve such problems was to create a world government.

From the start, this project was considered "utopian" by the politicians, who knew they would lose their positions if it caught on. The problem is the same for the members of the military with their fat pay checks, who are afraid of finding themselves unemployed. They know very well that with no borders, armies will no longer be needed, at least not in the way they think of them.

Actually, as we shall see later, there *will* be a way to employ these people. But unfortunately for those obsessed with shock commando tactics, no weapons will be needed by then.

It's always people of mediocre intelligence who accuse the geniuses' realistic projects of being utopian, simply because they can't see as far ahead as geniuses can. There's no such thing as a utopian project – just people incapable of realizing how such projects are feasible.

Therefore, the World Geniocratic Government will be composed of geniuses representing all regions of the world. These regions must first be democratically redefined, since most of our present-day borders are simply the result of murderous attacks by possessors

36

wishing to increase their riches. This practice dates back to colonial times.

The Basques who now live on both sides of the border between France and Spain might want to form their own state. That is their business and no one else's. It's up to them to decide whether they wish to be alone or be part of another state. And what applies to the Basques also applies to many other people around the world who live in particular regions and wish to have their own independent structures while being part of humanity as a whole. It's up to each of these regions to decide democratically about its structure, whether it's to be made up of Corsicans, Britons, Occitans or Alsatians – to mention just a few of the groups located on French territory.

Therefore, the inhabitants of every community should first vote democratically to establish which region they wish to be part of. That way, each region can be defined independent of any nationalist considerations. Moreover, this vote can be repeated whenever the inhabitants wish, since some bordering communities might wish to change regions in accordance with the movements of their people.

Once the regions are defined geographically by vote of the community inhabitants, each region can be divided into 12 sectors, each containing an equal number of inhabitants. Each sector will then elect one representative from its pool of geniuses, making a total of 12 elected geniuses to form the Regional Geniocratic College.

This regional college will elect its own president, who will represent the college at the World Geniocratic Government.

The Regional Geniocratic College will also elect a council of 12 creatives from the pool of creatives in its region. The function of this Regional Council of Creatives will be to submit creative projects relevant to its region for the college to vote on.

The World Geniocratic Government will therefore be composed of geniuses representing all the democratically defined regions of

Earth.

The vote of each regional representative will be weighed in proportion to the number of inhabitants living in that representative's region. For example, a genius representing a region of one million inhabitants will have a voting coefficient of 1, while a genius representing a region of 50 million inhabitants will have a voting coefficient of 50.

Therefore, unlike votes taking place in the United Nations, votes in the World Geniocratic Government will be truly democratic. How can the vote of a representative from a country such as Qatar, which has only 100,000 inhabitants, have the same value as that of the representative from the United States, which has more than 200 million inhabitants? Yet that's what is happening at the United Nations!

At any rate, if 700 regions define themselves democratically – a number that seems minimal for this world – then the college of the World Geniocratic Government will be composed of 700 geniuses from all races, cultures and religions. That's quite a different story than that of one mad genius intent on blowing up the planet!

II. Proposals for Turning Earth into a World of Happiness and Fulfillment

Warning

We have just explored the main principles of geniocracy. The basic principle is that only those of above-average intelligence have the right to vote, while only geniuses are eligible to govern.

Obviously, the way a geniocracy should be set up, including the definition of its structure and organization, is best decided by those involved – the geniuses themselves.

This book's only purpose is to spark the fuse that will lead to the explosion – in other words, to simply serve as the catalyst for a process that will be taken up and improved upon by those of above-average faculties. It would indeed be most presumptuous to attempt to tell the geniuses what decisions they are to make or how to govern the world. That will depend only on them.

The above examples of possible ways to organize the World Geniocratic Government are therefore just that – examples – and are in no way obligations. It would be very surprising if a group of a few hundred geniuses working together couldn't come up with even more appropriate solutions for this world.

In fact, the aim of this book is precisely that: to motivate the geniuses to unite so intelligence can finally govern our planet.

In the following pages, we'll turn our attention to the main problems facing humanity as it enters the Third Millennium, the dawn of which could be a Golden Age if the imbeciles presently in power can manage not to blow everything up before we even enter it.

Possible solutions will also be suggested. But once again, a group of geniuses will certainly find even more effective answers. Let them assemble, so that light may spring forth from their collective minds before our planet takes an irreversibly destructive turn.

To Workers Who Don't Enjoy Their Work

Humans are not made for doing forced labor. Yet you are all condemned to forced labor for life, with a pardon allowing you to be freed for retirement at 60 or 65.

What is the aim of all trade unions, and of workers themselves? Answer: to obtain shorter working hours. But how short? What is the acceptable length of daily forced labor for a human who wants to be free?

A century ago, people believed they had to work non-stop, apart from sleep and eating time. Workers were employed 14 hours a day, six days a week and 12 months a year – from the age of eight or nine until they died.

Then we went to 10 hours a day; then to eight hours a day and a five-day week – with a holiday period of one week per year; then to two, three and finally four weeks of holiday per year.

Retirement, which is the right to have enough to live on without having to do anything, was granted at 65, 60 and now – in some professions – at 55.

Flextime is becoming increasingly popular, giving people the possibility of managing their time of forced labor. So long as we do our 40 hours per week, we can choose the days and the times. Eight hours a day for five days, or 10 hours per day for four days, early morning or late at night.

What are the present trends, and where are they heading in the short term?

Some companies are already employing their work forces for less than eight hours a day: some for seven, some for six – and for four days a week instead of five. Some are even considering including in the eight-hour workday the two hours of commuting time Parisians need to get to and from work, thus bringing the workday down to six hours.

Many companies are already providing five-weeks of paid holidays per year, and an increasing number are taking that up to six weeks.

Companies are now attracting employees not with extravagant salaries, but with more flexible and shorter working hours, all in the name of "quality of life".

Many salaried or independent professionals are now "job-sharing", creating work teams reminiscent of those in liberal professions, such as doctors or lawyers sharing out patients and clients. Engineers or other highly skilled professionals share a salary and therefore need to work only four hours per day; or one week out of every two; or even five and a half months per year, giving each of them six and a half months of paid leave, since they are both getting a half-salary. During this "holiday", they can devote their time to any sort of activity, or even to work that is not forced upon them, such as research, writing books, studying, cultivating themselves, traveling, etc., and doing things they find fulfilling. More and more young executives are opting for a lower wage, such as three or four thousand francs per month instead of six to eight thousand. Although they may live slightly less luxuriously, they can do what they want for six months per year. Especially now that both men and women are working, if a couple wishes to live together, both half-salaries put together make one, if I'm not mistaken, giving them six months of paid holidays per year.

The same applies to retirement. Many people are choosing to stop working earlier, going on "pre-retirement" to enjoy more free time before they die – even if it means having a slightly lower pension. Of course, there are always exceptions, such as workaholics who have been so conditioned and depersonalized that they have no idea what they would do with their free time. Unfortunately for them, they can no longer conceive of their lives without work, and they have become incapable of fulfilling themselves in any area other than their job. This shows how much we need to adjust education to today's needs, so schools don't just turn out obedient workers, but people able to choose and fulfill themselves.

And what about tomorrow? As everyone can already see, working hours will continue to dwindle: from a six-hour day, to five hours, to four hours, to three....

Annual leave will increase: from a month and a half in summer, 15 days in winter and 15 days at Easter; to two months in summer, one month in winter and one month at Easter, resulting in a total of four months' leave per year. As job sharing becomes more popular, work time will diminish even more, giving job-sharing associates eight months of vacation per year, and retirement age will decrease: to 50, 45, 40....

"What will people do with their time?" you may well ask. The very question proves that your education has contaminated you and conditioned you into condemning yourself to a life sentence of forced labor. There will be two categories of people: those with a calling – a "gift" – who can fulfill themselves by working for pleasure in their particular fields during their leisure time and when they retire; and the others, who will enjoy all the cultural and sports activities adapted to each individual and provided by the full-leisure society.

As everyone's free time grows, the demand for writers, painters, poets, entertainers and all types of artists will increase to keep everyone enjoying the perpetual holidays. On one side will be the creators, and on the other the consumers, but everyone will be free to swap roles at any moment according to his or her own choice and taste.

After a certain amount of time (as soon as possible), as both working hours and the retirement age decrease, mandatory labor – forced labor – will be fully abolished. Only those who choose to work because they enjoy it will work, and work will therefore become *voluntary*. And so we will inscribe on the first line of the Declaration of Human Rights: *Every person has the unconditional right to receive the means to live comfortably from birth to death.*

"But who will take care of all the indispensable jobs?" you might ask.

The answer is: machines! Most people have no idea to what extent robots have already begun supporting humans in their work. The reason we're "already" working only eight hours a day is because of machines. Without them, we would still be doing the 10-hour day of 50 years ago.

For example, 20 years ago Fiat needed 100 workers to build a car. Now, with robots, only one human is needed. Yes, *just one human!* The new factory is fully automatic, with all the robots controlled by one central computer that just one human can supervise from the control room. But even that sole human technician will soon be replaced by a more sophisticated computer!

The same applies to agriculture: In California, for example, some agriculturists have set up a system in which their vines are maintained at optimum temperature, watered and fertilized – all automatically by a central computer.

Obviously, this system isn't viable in a capitalist society, since once owners automate their factories, they just fire all the workers without pay and let them starve while machines do all the work, filling the owners' pockets with gold from the profit. This is unjust and shouldn't be tolerated. The employer who builds a machine that replaces 100 workers should continue to pay these workers who now have nothing to do. The machine should thereby allow them to enter – and benefit from – the Age of Leisure.

People often say that machines enslave man and that technology dehumanizes society, but they're wrong! It's the manufacturer who enslaves man, and it's for the manufacturer that man is condemned to a life sentence of forced labor. The manufacturer enslaves us, but robots free us.

The only reason technology is dehumanizing society is that humans still have to work with the machines used for forced labor, or they have to "clock in" where the forced labor takes place. That is the problem: Humans and machines shouldn't be mixed together. Humans are designed to spend their time in places of fulfillment, while machines are designed to function in the workplace under the supervision of robots and computers.

Machines can replace every job done by man. Everything man does, a computer can do better. Man makes mistakes; computers don't.

If we took all the money presently tied up in military budgets worldwide and invested it in factories, production and workplaces, in seven years we could completely transform the world. All work could be entirely robotized, and humans would no longer be forced to work.

Humans are designed to fulfill themselves and machines are designed to work. The machine must do man's work rather than have humans do a machine's work – which is actually the case in most enterprises right now.

"And who would look after the machines?" you might ask.

The answer is very simple. In the short term, during the dozen or so years necessary for full robotization of all production, the military could maintain and manage the robots. Alternatively, we could create a type of civil service that would replace military service. Everyone would take turns working in it for only one or two years out of his or her life; or, as in the Swiss military service, everybody could just put in a period of about two weeks each year.

That way, only those called up – plus those who *wish* to do it all the time – would work on the production units, while everyone else could be entirely free. Of course, this arrangement would only be needed for a short transition period of about seven years, until fully robotized, self-maintaining, self-sufficient production units are set up. This is *the* future for humanity: one in which all production processes necessary for human life and fulfillment are maintained, monitored and repaired entirely by biological robots. This would apply to all areas: from agriculture to industry, domestic chores to art.

A biological robot is one made completely from living matter. We're just at the point of achieving such a robot right now through DNA synthesis.

If only the funds were made available to experts in cybernetics, biology and electronics, we would be able to create such biological robots very rapidly, and to design them with capabilities at least equal to man's at every level.

Evolution of Daily Working Hours and Changes in Beneficiaries

Unit of production	Means of existence	Daily working hours	Beneficiary	Means of exchange	Goal of activity
Tribe	Hunting and gathering	14 hours	The individual	Barter	Survival
Village	Animals and agriculture	14 hours	The individual	Money	Survival
Manufac-turer	Manual labor	14 hours	The boss	Money	Survival
Factory	Assisted manual labor	10 hours	The boss	Money	Survival
Semi-automated factory	Oversight and main-tenance	8 hours	The boss	Money	Living better
Fully automated factory	Nothing to do	0 hours	The collective	Distribu-tion	Fulfillment

49

How the Narrowing Salary Gap
Is Leading to a Moneyless Society

At the time of the financial aristocracy, when the lords exploited the surfs, the "salary gap" between them was about 1,000:1 for smaller lords; about 10,000:1 for important lords; and at least 100,000:1 for royalty in power.

Today, just taking France as an example, the salary gap is considerably smaller. It was rather brutally lowered during the Revolution, and after that a more progressive reduction culminated in the establishment of today's minimum wage. In present-day France, the equivalent of ruling royalty is the President of the Republic, who in 1977 – after taking into account all benefits of that job in terms of housing, transport, etc. – earns only about 30 times the minimum legal wage. So we can see that the salary gap has narrowed considerably in just the last 200 years, and it will continue to do so in the future.

Today's equivalent of the grand lord would be the government deputy or army general, or even the business executive, each of whom presently earns no more than about 15 times the minimum wage. There's no comparison with the 10,000-fold ratio of a few hundred years ago!

Finally, the small company boss, the comparable equivalent of a more minor lord, now earns no more than just seven times the minimum wage.

Every government in the world has on its agenda the goal of further reducing the salary gap, and the French government is aiming to lower it to 6:1. In Sweden, it has already gone down to 4:1, with the current aim of lowering it further, to only 3:1 – meaning no one would earn more than three times the minimum wage.

This process will continue around the world in parallel with the reduction of work time, so eventually there will be no salary gap at all. And once there's no salary gap, it's obvious that money will cease to be useful, and at that point it can be removed permanently without any problems. Around that time, all of us will probably adopt this universal principle: *Everyone has the right to receive everything necessary to live comfortably from birth to death, without preconditions.*

A Distributive Economy

The first step toward dismantling today's "life-sentence-of-forced-labor system" lies in creating a distributive economy, which removes the necessity for money.

A distributive economic system is based on the principle that we only produce what people need – no more, no less.

Man's basic needs include:
- Food
- Clothing
- Housing

Society must provide these three elements unconditionally.

And this must be done on a world scale rather than simply on a national level, since nations as we know them will no longer exist.

If all food, clothing and housing production is handled by computers and robots, and provided free to everyone – regardless of race, function, religion or sex – then things with intrinsic value will be appreciated for their real value, while things that were simply expensive will fade away.

For example, artists will be able to paint what they wish without having to worry about whether it will sell well or not. Instead, they can offer their work to friends who would really appreciate it rather than have other people buy it as an investment, or for snobbish reasons.

As soon as an invention is considered interesting, however impractical it may be, it can be automatically produced and distributed to everyone who wants it. Thus the criteria of commercial viability will no longer block creativity.

And what about collector's items? Well, the twenty-first century won't have collector's items, except for human genius. Everything will be easily reproducible. Whether it's to be caviar, champagne, diamonds, wine, meat, gemstones or perfumes, it's composed of chemicals that can be synthesized in laboratories. Even life – including man, who is basically a molecule of DNA that contains the personality within its genetic code – is reproducible.

Work and Prostitution

"For centuries, forced labor has been breaking our bones,
bruising our flesh and weighing on our nerves; for centuries,
hunger has been torturing our guts and hallucinating our brains!
O laziness, take pity on our long misery! O lazybones, mother
of the arts and noble virtues, be the comforter of our anxiety!"

Paul Lafargue

Both the laborers who are behind their machines eight hours a day, and the clerks, who spend the same amount of time blackening paper with ink, look down on prostitutes – yet there's not much difference between all of them.

The prostitute rents the use of her body a few minutes a day for money, while the laborer and the salaried employee rent theirs for eight hours a day to a boss. So does the engineer, who in fact sells the use of both his body and his mind for money. The truth is that all who work in exchange for a salary are prostituting themselves one way or another.

I knew a well-educated young woman with a postgraduate university degree who was prostituting herself on the Champs-Elysées in Paris. Her reasoning went like this:

"I have a heap of diplomas, and the jobs they entitle me to work at would allow me to earn just enough to live on while teaching the philosophy of Nietzsche to future greengrocers

54

– but without any time to myself, or any time to fulfill my passion for writing. But by prostituting my body one or two hours a day, I can earn an enormous amount of money and still have time to devote myself to my books and my philosophy the rest of the day. Given a choice between prostituting my mind or my body, I didn't hesitate one moment...."

Here is reasoning one can't argue with. Unfortunately, the rest of us "prostitute-for-life" workers aren't lucky enough to have a body as beautiful as hers, or even so lucid a mind. That's why we must unite and demand that a geniocratic government be implemented – so that geniuses will replace mental and physical prostitutes with machines and computers, thereby removing the necessity for money and prostitution.

THE WORKERS OF TOMORROW:
ELECTRONIC OR BIOLOGICAL ROBOTS

*"We would no longer need slaves if tools
could move by themselves."*

ARISTOTLE

In the next few years, the integration of electronics, cybernetics, computer science and biology will allow us to create robots that can do all our work faster and more precisely than we can.

The newest generation of computers is already far superior to humans in terms of information storage and data analysis.

Also, the field of computer-aided instruction is expanding rapidly. For example, programs already train medical students by first describing theoretical symptoms and prompting students to make a diagnosis, then commenting on their replies just as a real teacher would. It would be no problem to connect such a computer to a series of sensors to measure temperature, heart rate and blood pressure, and even to do blood and urine analysis, thereby automatically giving the patient a full medical examination – with no need for the presence of other humans.

The problem of communication between computers and humans has also been solved. Some recently available programs synthesize the human voice, enabling computers to communicate information orally, just as humans do, rather than merely present text on a screen.

Equipped with a voice analyzer, such a machine can "listen" to spoken information and respond to it. This capacity opens up interactive possibilities. For example, the computer might ask, "Does it hurt when I press you here?" or advise, "Please relax," when it detects high muscular tension in the patient. In fact, it could even be equipped with a voice more soothing than that of many human doctors, whose vocal chords are often stressed and tense.

As you can see, the future utility of robots is far more sophisticated and far-reaching than merely using them for the automated construction of cars on an assembly line. And we're not talking science fiction. These developments are occurring right now, today. As usual, fact surpasses fiction by far. Everything that humans do, machines can do – or soon will do – better and faster, and I do mean everything.

This statement even applies to art and creativity, which for a long time were believed to be exclusively human capabilities.

Indeed, programs that can compose – and even play – their own music are already being used. And everyone is familiar with the synthesizers used more and more often in popular music. But sequencer/samplers – essentially computerized synthesizers – can now reproduce all the sounds of any musical instrument, including the human voice.

Such a machine can be programmed to play a piece by Bach or Beethoven, and with far more precision than any symphony orchestra in the world can attain. Imagine an orchestra of 100 violins. Such a large number of human violinists would never be able to strike a string with the bow at exactly the same time. A time lag of a few tenths of a second between the first violin and the last is unavoidable, as well as a few hundredths of a second between those coming in between. On the other hand, a computer can be programmed for all violins to start together, down to a millionth of a second. The resulting synchronicity of sound is far better than even the greatest human conductor can hope to achieve.

And should you think it's that very time lag or minute human hesitation that gives an orchestra or conductor unique character, know that the same time lag can also be programmed in, allowing the computer to achieve that identical character.

Another advantage of the computerized synthesizer is that it can produce much purer sounds than the original acoustic instruments, which are dependent on conditions and natural acoustics of the room in which they are played. The difference is particularly obvious when we have to record the sounds of acoustic instruments through microphones and then project those sounds through amplifiers. Using a synthesizer, the electronic signals can be directly recorded in pure form, with no loss of any quality due to acoustic defects of the room in which the recording takes place.

Jean-Claude Risset, composer and head of research at the *Centre National de la Recherche Scientifique*, says: "There is no limit to the precision and virtuosity of the computer, which can execute difficult musical pieces and complex rhythms with an exactitude inaccessible to human performers. Some composers prefer to use the computer rather than human performers."[2]

And whatever is possible in the realm of sound is equally feasible with colors, shapes, perfumes and tastes.

When an artist reproduces the ideal curved line of a hip, it's just one drawn line out of an infinite number of possibilities. The computer can do that too. In fact, it can even be programmed to include the "mistakes" that give some painters a distinctive style, such as Modigliani's long necks or Buffet's large number of vertical lines. And just as the computer can reproduce Modigliani's style, it can also be programmed to compose music in the style of Bach.

A computer can even "discover" a style that doesn't yet exist by checking out all existing styles and inventing one that best corresponds to the taste of a particular audience.

As Professor Arnold Kaufman of the *Institut Polytechnique National de Grenoble* put it, "The role of the computer in the creative process is just in its infancy and shows great promise."[2] And recent developments prove that reality is already surpassing his predictions.

Moreover, if computers can successfully take on such delicate and subtle specialities as the arts, then it's easy to see how they can also take care of all our basic needs – such as food, energy and the production of goods – without the slightest problem.

When all production is automated, the creation of such computers and robots will be an important step in this process. This could take a lot of time and energy unless we design computers capable of completing their own production. Somewhat the way a human body builds itself according to instructions contained in the genetic code of its first cell – and building its own eyes, arms, etc. – a central computer could be given a complete plan that would enable it to build extensors and sensors for each model it makes.

It might even be possible to include data in the program of the central computer that would enable it to reproduce and create other central computers, which themselves could also reproduce, just as humans with their genital organs can create other humans, who in turn will be able to do the same thing. For auto-reproducing computers, there will be "conservation of the model" rather than conservation of the species.

Though the use of metal in robots will in no way impair their efficiency in areas of food, energy and goods production, for robot work requiring close proximity to humans – such as domestic work within our homes – machines with a more harmonious texture will be required. Right now, we can easily conceive of "intelligent houses" that would clean themselves automatically and respond to all needs of their inhabitants, including food, hygiene and entertainment. Such houses would be able to prepare meals according to the vocal instructions of the homeowner; fill the bath at the correct temperature and level; and turn the TV on to the requested channel; but it's much more likely that we would choose to be looked after by autonomous robot servants that look human.

That's where biology comes in.

Humans find contact with metallic entities to be lacking in "warmth", and will therefore create biological robots: robots made from living matter and programmed to do what we ask of them.

Surely some people will object, saying we have no right to create intelligent living slaves. But computers are also "living" entities gifted with intelligence.

Does the fact of being made of living biological material change the problem, given that we can synthesize this living matter?

What's more, slavery means forcing living organisms to work against their will, under threat of the whip or of food deprivation. But the creation of biological robots genetically programmed to work and obey human wishes means they can't conceive of anything else, and they therefore do this work entirely voluntarily, just as humans eat, drink and sleep entirely voluntarily. Thus there is nothing to liberate them from.

But if we make these biological robots look human, we'll need to give them some sort of physical mark, so we can tell the difference between them and humans: either something hereditary, or a necklace they will always wear, or something like a stone encrusted in their foreheads.

Biological robots could be mass-produced like other computers, so they could be immediately usable but incapable of self-reproducing; or they could be programmed to self-reproduce by sexual reproduction or simple division.

And to help the anti-robot-slavery puritans pass painlessly through the psychological shock, it might help to avoid giving the first few generations of robots a too-human appearance. Seeing "slaves" with dog-like heads would probably shock them much less than seeing them with human-like heads. Nevertheless, it would be much more pleasant to spend time with "slaves" who look like Alain Delon and Brigitte Bardot!

ELIMINATION OF MONEY:
THE RETURN TO REAL VALUES

In today's society, the value we put on people is often in proportion to how much money they have. Whether they're writers, painters, inventors, musicians or researchers, if they're penniless, nobody is interested in them. As a society, we put financial worth before personal value, and for reinforcement we say, "We only lend to the rich."

We put net worth above personal worth not only when granting – or not granting – financial loans, but also when deciding whether or not to pay attention to someone. No one is interested in the artistic genius exposing his wares in the streets, but when the same painter shows his works in a famous gallery, all the women are endlessly excited by them. Musicians and poets fare a similar fate: As far as most of our contemporaries are concerned, the god of money is the only one worth adoring.

I have a friend who is just beginning to be recognized as one of today's great painters. He explained to me the process his agent used to get him known around the world so that people would be prepared to pay their weight in gold to obtain one of his paintings.

First, he convinced a famous movie star to buy one of the paintings by saying it would be "an extraordinary investment" (again, money!). Next, he gave a few paintings as gifts to the most influential journalists at the largest papers, stressing that in a week's time the value of these works would rise so much that they could be sold for a vast profit. In return, he asked the journalists to launch the young prodigy by writing about the famous movie star's interest in him.

The wheels were set in motion, and other papers soon followed suit, singing praises about the paintings that were "selling like hot-cakes". The buzz in the newspapers led to further publicity on television, and finally the agent was able to persuade moguls of finance to buy "the few remaining paintings" before their prices rose too much. He sold them the paintings he had in the interim bought back from the journalists, who were only too happy to oblige.

The few hundred remaining paintings the agent had kept in reserve sold rapidly, gaining value by their own momentum. Soon everyone wanted one of these now-famous works of art, which the media were by then comparing to Picasso's.

But in the meantime, my friend saw none of the profits and earned only a fixed salary from the agent – just enough to live on – in return for producing a certain number of paintings per year under the terms of a three-year contract.

Obviously, this arrangement was better for the artist than starving under the bridges of Montmartre. But this example illustrates how the process of creating fame and artistic repute isn't based for even one moment on the emotions induced by works of art, but founded solely on money and profit.

My friend, who will remain anonymous, is perfectly aware of the monstrosity of this system. He continues to provide the 25 paintings stipulated in his contract, even though he runs them off in one weekend and in a completely artificial style not of his own choosing. He does this so he can spend the rest of the year painting the things he really likes, which he keeps for himself. When his contract is over, he will exhibit his real works of art, but this arrangement shows what indirect and obscure routes must be taken for genius to be recognized.

When we finally live in a moneyless society, painters, musicians, inventors and researchers will be able to do what they really love. The only people lucky enough to have an original painting from the artists of the time will be not those whose only merit is having a big fat bank account, but those who with so much warmth and emotion feel the depth of what the artist is trying to express. The artist will give his works to them out of friendship.

That is when things will be appreciated for their real values. No longer will we try to blind the gallery with a collection paid for with a king's ransom. Those able to build up a collection will not have been able to do so because they had plenty of money, but because they were those who most appreciated and understood the artists and gave them the most warmth, friendship and impartial encouragement.

The religion of personal value will replace the religion of money. And artists will have followings made up of fans and admirers who are there because the art fills them with joy and enthusiasm, as does the thought of living alongside the artists and being the first to see their creations take shape.

What a lot of things we will have to learn – especially those of us who only know how to have, who have never tried just being.

When money has been abolished, we will truly understand why it was written, "The first shall be the last."

THE MOST DANGEROUS SECT OF ALL: THE ARMY

The society of tomorrow must be non-violent, and people must be able to fulfill themselves in a culture of tolerance. Everyone must have the right to be different in every way, including his or her religious, sexual and political orientation, etc.

There must be no more religious, sexual, political or ethnic prejudice. We must stop behaving like primitives and cease being afraid of others who are different, or who have chosen to be different.

A cult is just someone else's religion.

Vice is just someone else's sensuality.

We must be aware of these things to become more tolerant.

Christians must not forget that only 2,000 years ago, they themselves would have been considered members of a dangerous cult, and may even have been thrown to the lions. Therefore, they have no right to label the new religions of today as cults, especially when those new religions give meaning to the lives of so many young people.

If my neighbor starts proclaiming that his belly button is the center of the world, and this belief helps thousands of people, then those thousands of people should be free to build a golden throne in his honor if it pleases them – especially when, being tolerant themselves, they realize that not everyone shares their belief.

If someone else's faith bothers you, it's because you're unsure of your own conception of life and the universe.

The same principle applies to sexuality. If a man's or woman's natural sexual rhythm is three times per day, we shouldn't accuse that person of sexual perversion just because we only need to make love once a week. Everyone has his or her own rhythm.

Vice is just someone else's sensuality.

And assuming someone is brainwashed because his or her religion differs from the major traditional faiths constitutes not only a serious lack of tolerance, but the first step toward the labor camps of totalitarian states.

If we can't accept that others may freely choose their own religion without questioning their mental health or spiritual balance, we're falling back to the medieval trappings of the Inquisition. But this time, torture has been replaced by more subtle techniques of mental alienation, and by restriction of choice and responsibility through medical control and internment in psychiatric hospitals. In other words, we're reverting to "Gulags" for spiritual and religious "dissidents" in our so-called free countries.

In the U.S.S.R., brainwashing and internment were rationalized as necessary measures for solving the so-called "problem" of dissidents who no longer agreed with the political system. But some people in today's *non-totalitarian* states dare to suggest the same brainwashing techniques for treating those no longer in agreement with the major traditional religions.

People are quick to talk about the moral and even physical violence the new religions (usually pejoratively referred to as "cults") supposedly inflict upon their new adepts. But nobody ever mentions the largest institution of brainwashing and physical and moral violence that has ever existed – the military.

What is the young conscript subjected to?

First, he undergoes major depersonalization through various physical modifications: haircut, uniform, clothing, etc.

66

Next, after his own personality has been repressed, he is told how to behave. New behavior patterns are imprinted through physical exercises designed to establish automatic reflex behavior, such as marching, saluting and reacting violently to the approach of a stranger.

Meanwhile, any opportunity to think for himself or remember his old self is prevented through a never-ending series of trivial tasks, very little rest, insufficient nourishment and food of poor quality (and low in protein to make the brain more sensitive to discipline). Moral violence, unfair punishments, lack of choice and continual physical harassment against which he can do nothing (superiors instigating these measures are "always right") all reinforce the brainwashing process.

Therefore, if we're to talk about brainwashing, we mustn't forget to mention the biggest den of this iniquity, the military. We must see it for what it really is: an establishment of hyper-conditioning, in which everything is organized in such a way that young conscripts have nothing to think about or worry about and can just devote themselves to automatically obeying orders without question. The idea is to make robots of them – robots who will automatically kill anyone, anywhere, when given the order. In fact, they would even go so far as to release bombs on cities containing several million inhabitants. That is the basis of this brainwashing process.

Right now there are young people all over the world who have been so deeply conditioned by the military that they wouldn't hesitate one moment to pull the trigger and kill millions of innocent people – just because they were given the order.

That is where you can find real brainwashing, not in "cults".

The process for conditioning the young people employed by the military is simple and eloquent:

1) Depersonalization;
2) Behavioral imprinting;
3) Control and maintenance of required personality.

It's quite amazing to see how many young people let themselves be seduced into the professional army after being given food, lodging and almost constant repetitive tasks for their 12 months of military service. Their fear of returning to civilian life shows just how many young people have been conditioned and rendered incapable of doing anything other than obeying orders, let alone thinking for themselves.

A good example is all those O.A.S. veterans from Indochina: the old Legionnaires and the former American Marines, who were so conditioned that they found it difficult to readapt to civilian life, and instead turned to violence and crime.

A geniocratic government must study this problem so that such brainwashing will no longer be organized by society.

It's also very revealing that many war criminals – such as the old Nazis – always try to hide behind the excuse that they were "only obeying orders". Those who tortured the Soviet dissidents would certainly say the same thing to defend themselves if judged, and so would those who displayed such violence in Algeria, Indochina and Vietnam – or even those who dropped the bomb on Hiroshima.

They are all basically the same.

The military is the No. 1 enemy of the people because its members are all irresponsible, and they even proclaim their lack of responsibility at the first opportunity. What is most serious is that they transform young, responsible people into assassins ready to carry out the most hideous crimes at the slightest order, and who know that when questioned later for their actions, they can always hide behind the excuse that they were just following orders.

For a society to be morally clean, it must ensure that all people in it be acutely aware that they themselves will be held personally responsible for every act of violence they carry out, under any circumstances, and that obeying an order implies a responsibility just as large as that of the one giving it.

When an assassin is hired to kill someone, can that assassin be excused on the grounds that he was just obeying orders?

Surely it's not too much to hope for that our society be composed of responsible individuals, whatever their functions.

Each person taking part in a firing squad is just as guilty as the person ordering the firing. Only when everyone is capable of refusing to carry out inhuman acts – without hiding behind uniforms or functions – can we hope for universal peace.

In the same way, every judge and every jury that condemns an innocent person should – once the latter has been able to prove his innocence – be condemned to a sentence equal to the one inflicted unjustly, or at least a sentence equal to the one that already has been served by the victim of such injustice. This will make judges and juries – who sometimes make judgments out of intolerance and unfounded "personal convictions" – think twice before pronouncing their justice.

HOW TO SILENCE THE MILITARY

Imagine if the scientists living after the 1914 war had not given the fruit of their research to the political-military powers at that time, but instead had pooled them together in a neutral state. By 1935, they would have found themselves with sufficient technology to completely crush conventional armies, which had hardly progressed at all, and the war of 1939-1945 would have been avoided. Hitler would not have had the V1 and V2 rockets and the United States would not have had the atomic bomb. Only the center of world peace would have had such technology and could even have decided to use it against the Nazi tyrant before he caused too much damage.

The United Nations is powerless to achieve anything, since its Blue Helmets are only an army for political dissuasion, and their equipment is insignificant compared to that of the superpowers.

On the other hand, if scientists – the true instigators of technological development – were to ally now for peace, the aforementioned example of 1914-1935 could come about rapidly. We could just as well have taken as an example the days of steel weapons, during which wars were fought with swords, bows and arrows. If the scientists who developed gunpowder and pistols had gotten together instead of being manipulated by the political-military powers, they could have prevailed and installed peace.

The same can be said of the 1870-1914 period. If the scientists had gotten together then to exploit their early discoveries in the automotive field and in aviation, they could have prevented the 1914-18 war by reducing its protagonists to silence.

But our biggest concern is the present, which will determine humanity's future. Though the armies of today appear to possess incredibly advanced weaponry, if our scientists were to get together now, they could develop far more sophisticated technology. Within the next 10 years, they could make the armies' pride look like kid's toys compared to what they would develop, giving them the leverage to impose universal peace right down to the last bastions of the recalcitrant political-military powers.

Since it was the scientists who invented the technology used by the military to make today's weapons, they would also have no difficulty inventing ways to neutralize such weapons and render them useless. In fact, they could even create non-violent weapons, such as paralyzing waves that last just a few hours – time enough for commandos of the non-violent World Army to enter every country and disarm all stockpiles of nuclear and bacteriological weapons.

FOR THE CREATION OF A GENETIC IDENTITY CARD

"If we wish to prevent the human race from degenerating,
we must be careful to encourage unions between the
best specimens and rarefy those between the worst."

PLATO

Selection or degeneration: These are the only two options for all living species, including man.

Either humanity will establish some sort of genetic self-selection or it will degenerate.

Natural selection exists for all animal species, just as it did for man before science and medicine short-circuited the process. Today, natural selection of man no longer exists, and man has already started to degenerate. The only way to halt this degeneration is to replace natural selection with artificial selection. This must not be done on living subjects – as the Nazi criminals attempted – but genetically, before the child is conceived.

Prenuptial examinations are already an established process designed to define the risks of bearing handicapped children. This is good, but not sufficient. What we need is a genetic and chromosomal identity card indicating the characteristics, illnesses, deformations and genetic mutations of ancestors up to seven generations back.

When partners want to have a child, they could put their genetic cards together. By using a computer to compare their respective hereditary traits, a specialist would be able to tell them the probability of having a handicapped child.

If the chances are above a certain threshold, it wouldn't be advisable for the couple to have a child by natural means. Instead, they could have one either by artificial insemination of the mother's egg with healthy sperm, or by implantation of a healthy egg fertilized by the father's sperm.

We have no problem selecting plants and animals, yet we shrink away completely at the idea of selection for humans. However, one day we will have to do it – or we will degenerate, slowly but surely.

EDUCATION

"Everyone complains about their memory,
but no one complains about their judgment."

LA ROCHEFOUCAULD

Under the present mediocratic system, we give exactly the same education to a potential genius that we give to an imbecile. The sole outcome is that young geniuses – who can understand in minutes what might take others days, weeks, months or even years to assimilate – get bored and put off their studies. Yet since school syllabi are designed for the average student, the gifted are left to waste their time doing all the endless repetitions necessary for mediocre students. No wonder they become totally disinterested.

Here, too, geniocracy needs to intervene. It must evaluate the intelligence of children at various ages to cull the geniuses and the gifted, then educate them according to their own levels. Children can be tested at age five, when they enter school, and at 12, when they enter secondary school.

If you think about it, it's rather astounding that more resources are devoted to the education of the mentally handicapped than to the gifted. This is revealing: it shows that those in charge – the guardians of mediocrity – are very much afraid of those whose intelligence is above average.

In fact, Russia and America have already taken steps to see that genius isn't wasted: They've established special schools for the gifted, and those schools are already producing fantastic results. Unfortunately, they're still too rare. And apart from the two superpowers mentioned, the rest of the world – under the sterile and meaningless pretext of egalitarianism – refuses to consider such education for super-brains.

This is an irreparable crime. With such slow and mediocre education, how many geniuses have been held back, kept from using and developing their brains at their own faster pace? Not only have they have been turned off to studies, but their brains have atrophied from lack of challenge.

Another point worth reforming in education is the exaggerated importance placed on memory, and to the detriment of what really characterizes true human intelligence – imagination.

For many years, these young brains are stuffed full of facts they have to learn "by heart". And while they are busy learning that way, their memories are certainly developing, but not their intelligence. Any old computer can accumulate knowledge, but the human brain should be trained to imagine, not to memorize.

In some Chinese schools, students are already taking "open book exams". In other words, they can refer to books and notes when answering the examiner's questions. This trains them to synthesize information, which is much more useful than simply memorizing it.

In the days of the quill pen, how many children had their learning time wasted by plume fanatics? Such teachers spent countless hours obsessing about how to write without splashing the ink. Now everyone uses ballpoint pens.

We have similar fanatics today, except this time they poison children's minds by obsessing about equations. In a world of pocket calculators, who needs them? In fact, these little machines are already allowed in new American schools, just as typewriters are. We must allow that same progress everywhere else.

THE STATUS OF WOMEN AND OF PEOPLE IN DEVELOPING COUNTRIES

Geniocracy is concerned with human beings, not genders. So at first sight, devoting an entire chapter to the subject of women's status could be construed as a form of sexism in itself. But since misogyny as a phenomenon is still so widespread, I feel it's important to take issue with it.

One might be tempted to say that a geniocratic government should be 50 percent male and 50 percent female, but that would be wrong, for gender is irrelevant. The only important factor is intelligence. While men strut about flaunting their muscular superiority – a rather irrelevant characteristic as far as our civilization is concerned – in the really useful domain of intelligence, women might even have a slight edge.

Only time will tell after the tests are developed, but even if the world government is one day 75 percent or even 100 percent female, so long as those women actually are more intelligent than average, I would consider it truly just. However, we have to be very careful in ensuring that psychologists of both sexes develop the tests, so that the tests are truly "asexual".

The same applies to people in developing countries. At first, we might be tempted to design special tests adapted to what some people call "primitives". However, that would be a mistake since, as mentioned earlier, the only criteria is intelligence. People shouldn't say that we should shelter such people from civilization to conserve their true identity.

Like all living organisms, ethnic minorities – groups well behind our own civilization's development – will have to either adapt or die, unless they want to be conserved in their primitive state in those terrible human zoos known as reservations.

The idea of having India and Biafra send out mercy missions to reduce human suffering and starvation in the French Massif Central region or New York might seem ridiculous, but the fact that it doesn't happen is proof enough that Western Civilization is better at solving these problems. And it's no coincidence that countries based on this civilization are now rich, while developing countries use them as a model.

Allowing certain ethnic minorities to continue their barbaric customs is a crime against women, even if it's done on the pretext of respecting their traditions. French television recently showed a tribe that still considers women to be unclean and inferior. They're allowed only the most poorly placed houses and the worst food, and they're forbidden to enter the men's section.

If we knew of a tribe practicing slavery, we would try to put an end to it immediately, wherever on earth it might be, but since the only victims of this segregation are women, we turn a blind eye to it. And to top it off, we support it out of "respect for these tribal customs".

This is intolerable! No one on Earth has the right to practice such sexual discrimination, and we have the right to put an end to it wherever it is hiding – and that includes Western Civilization, of course!

As the poet once said, "Women are man's future", and I'm sure whoever said that was right. For the violent world bequeathed to us today is the fruit of a succession of almost exclusively male governments. Perhaps it's a sign from above that just when men are getting ready to blow everything up, women are starting to have their say. In other words, we could translate the poet's phrase into, "Women are humanity's future."

What's certain is that a woman would never have given the order to drop the bomb on Hiroshima, nor sent the V1s to London, nor ordered the fabrication of bacterial weapons. Women have a greater respect for life – perhaps because they give birth to it, perhaps because they're brought up in a way that doesn't glorify strength – but the results speak for themselves. Women's demonstrations in Northern Ireland provide evidence that women will be one of the principal levers in establishing universal peace.

DEMOGRAPHY

*"If throughout the world, undesired children were
never conceived, the problem of overpopulation
would be solved to a large extent."*

THE VICE PRESIDENT OF THE POPULATION COUNCIL

The days of, "Go forth and multiply," are over. There is no room left! Thankfully, for the first time in history, man has the means to curb his population growth.

An irresponsible few continue to complain because the people of France, among others, have understood how important lowering the birth rate is for happiness – and, indeed, for survival. Those opposed to the reduction justify their cause with the classic excuse: *Our neighboring country's population is multiplying so fast that it will one day outnumber us. Therefore, our neighbor constitutes a threat.*

What they don't realize is that if countries continue to compete economically (and this sort of competition rather than co-operation is something we must strive to avoid), the least populated will be most likely to do best. The reason is simple: They will have fewer mouths to feed while robotization makes up for lost labor.

1976 was a milestone year for France. For the first time in all its history, its population stopped increasing and even decreased slightly.

We need to encourage the world's youth to have fewer children.

However, they're being fed the argument that if they do, there won't be enough young to feed the old.

That isn't true! The world of automation is approaching fast, and the parents of today are building a world where their children will no longer have to work to feed them.

Also, women need to start making themselves heard, and to stop allowing themselves to be exploited by pill pushers growing rich at their expense.

A vaccine recently designed to replace the contraceptive pill lasts from one to three years, and without the pill's negative side effects. The catch is that the pharmaceutical laboratories have decided to reserve it solely for developing countries. While the vaccine's cost is relatively minor, the conventional pill is a gold mine of profit for the manufacturers because of its daily use! We mustn't stand for such a situation, in which financial interests deprive women of such an essential discovery simply because it has the disadvantage of being too cheap!

Justice

Justice is another area in which geniocracy must be respected. How can we accept that one man judges another without being sure the judge is more intelligent? Is it conceivable that a genius be judged by fools? Yet that is happening right now, and unfortunately it has always been this way.

Only those able to vote should have the right to judge petty criminals. And for major crimes, juries should be selected from among the eligibles – in other words, from the pool of geniuses.

As for sentencing, punishments are now more like revenge than a practical way to prevent crime. You can't cure criminals by putting them in prison; it only hardens or makes them bitter. Instead, scientific means are available to heal people who have become guilty of violence.

Doctor Heinz Lehman of McGill University discovered a chemical naturally existing in the brain that normally suppresses excess aggression and thus reduces violence. It would be much more reasonable to condemn violent criminals to treatment with this drug, which, in contrast to prison, will really have a positive effect on them.

In fact, it would be even more preferable to prevent criminality rather than intervene after the act is done. Maybe we could envisage measuring the chemical level of aggression in adolescents and correct it with doses of the anti-aggression chemical before they could commit terrible crimes.

Some might call this brainwashing, but isn't that precisely what a society is aiming to do by imprisoning its criminals for 10 to 20 years? By doing so, isn't our society trying to modify criminal tendencies and change the personalities of killers through long and painful brainwashing that in the end proves useless? A chemical treatment, the effects of which can be regularly monitored, would be notably less barbaric than years in a cell.

ADOLESCENT MARTYRS

I'm not talking about abused children, at least not exclusively. The point is to ensure that everyone already be developed and fulfilled by the 18th birthday (which is when they will be allowed to vote). To that end, they will need to have experienced intimacy for at least four years beforehand. In other words, from the age of 14, adolescents have the right to a sexual, political and religious life independent from their parents.

Therefore, we must recognize that adolescents have the right to their own sexual lives – a freedom enabled by today's contraceptives – and we must remove laws that criminalize sexual activity between someone over the age of 18 and someone under that age.

We must also allow adolescents to consult gynecologists alone – without their parents – and without it costing them anything, and give them the freedom to choose freely whether they want to use contraceptives or not.

We must also permit them to participate in any religious or political organization without a parent's consent.

We must prohibit all forms of corporal punishment, whether from parents or educators, for those over 14.

We must recognize that adolescents have the right to choose their own physical appearance, which means they must be free to choose their own clothes, hairstyle, etc.

We must establish communities where adolescents who feel uncomfortable at home can come and live without parental authorization.

We must allow adolescents to choose which parent they want to live with if the parents divorce.

We must recognize the right for adolescents to choose whether they want to go to boarding school or not.

We must stop using report cards for adolescents.

THE CREATION OF CENTERS OF DEVELOPMENT

We must establish centers for fulfillment and the awakening of body and mind in all regions and main cities of the world so all can fulfill themselves to their full potential.

Certain people who couldn't fulfill themselves because of blockages stemming from family environment will be able to free themselves of those blockages and therefore achieve their full potential at these centers, perhaps enabling them to become electors, or even better, to become eligibles when they pass the tests seven years later.

In these centers, under the guidance of specialists, psychologists, sexologists and philosophers, people will be able to progress along the path of self-discovery by removing false ideas and opening their minds to infinity through the use of various meditation techniques.

Sexuality, the primary factor in psychological blockage, should be given priority, and sensuality even more so.

Since money will be abolished more or less in the long term, human beings will one day have to be able to satisfy their sexuality freely, without the slightest complex.

The centers could be the key to totally eliminating prostitution. Both men and women could meet freely at such centers and enjoy sexual relations of reciprocal consent with no strings attached other than the pleasure they give to each other. Psychologists and sexologists could help those having the most problems in determining their preferences and help them find partners with the same preferences.

86

It would even be desirable for sex education to be taught there. Incidentally, schoolteachers now either avoid providing sex education or do it very badly because of shame and inhibitions about their own sexuality. In the centers, specialists could teach not only the "colder" facts of "how sex works", but also present its warm and sensual aspects so students learn how to both enjoy it and give pleasure, which is much more important and fulfilling.

This sensual education could first be taught as theory. Then, for those who desire it, it could become practical in the context of adolescents having the right to enjoy their own sexual lives. Freely and independently, they could choose consenting partners, or, if they wish, learn under the supervision of specialists – with all the guarantees and advantages that would contribute to both physical and psychological development.

In this way, almost all violent or clumsy acts that have completely and irreversibly traumatized young girls and ignorant young people could be almost fully eradicated.

Such instruction would also eliminate today's huge number of unwanted pregnancies that end up as abortions or worse, completely wasting the youth of young girls with such a premature family burden.

Finally, the development of venereal diseases – a scourge of our time mainly because about 80 percent of young men have their first sexual experience with a prostitute – will be almost completely eliminated. Modern contraception can allow young people to stay healthy while discovering the joys of sex, without the slightest risk and with partners freely chosen from their own circles rather than from the sordid world of prostitution.

Back to Nature, Thanks to Science

Some people think they have to shun science to get back to nature and restore their freedom and communication with the natural elements. Well, that is a mistake!

In the beginning, humans had to fight the ravages of nature to survive. That's all they were concerned with every moment of the day, every day of their lives. It took them hours to make even the simplest of tools for hunting or fishing – and for agricultural tools, it took even longer.

Then the industrial age arrived, and humans had to spend their time in factories or offices. There, though far removed from nature, they were able for the first time to have a few hours each day, and even some months per year, during which they didn't have to concentrate purely on survival. Everyday chores were lightened, thanks to the use of household inventions. Instead of having women spend three hours a week on their hands and knees scrubbing laundry clean in cold water, all we have to do now is simply put some powder in a machine and press the button. To refuse science and progress also means refusing the benefits they have brought us – and going back to our hands and knees.

If some men still feel nostalgic for old times, it's because they never had to scrub the wash themselves. And if some women want to go back, it's because they don't know what it was really like. For them, it is the country, their little goat and potatoes in the garden and their little country cottage that they only go to on weekends.

But when we refuse science and progress, little goats have to be milked by hand every morning at the crack of dawn, and we have to cut their straw for winter – also by hand – and dig up the potatoes, again by hand – and that's after having to cut wood to keep warm, sew clothes to wear and do other tasks, leaving not one minute to read, write, paint, go to the cinema or do anything entertaining or fulfilling.

No, instead of wanting to turn back the clock, we should continue on the road of scientific progress. It will eventually allow humanity to return back to nature – not to be dominated by it, but to enjoy it – and without the disadvantage of having to scrape out a living.

When work becomes completely automated and the need for money is removed, humans can return to nature and live within it. They will have no need to do anything other than simply commune with nature and fulfill themselves in harmony with the elements.

At that time, those who wish to breed goats and plant potatoes will be able to do so freely, not because they have to feed their children, but simply because they get fulfillment from it.

FOR THE CREATION OF A WORLD LANGUAGE

One of the most important elements needed for establishing a true union of all people on Earth is the creation of a world language. Not a universal language – because the world is not the universe – but a world language.

A few candidates, including Esperanto, have already been proposed. Unfortunately, they have all been rooted in Greek and Latin and are thereby totally unacceptable for Asians, who represent over half of humanity. What do the Chinese and Japanese care about Latin roots?

No, the only realistic way to create a true world language acceptable to all people on Earth is to create a completely new language, the learning of which will put no one at a disadvantage. That is to say, it shouldn't be rooted in any of today's languages, which means it must be totally new.

We must bring the top linguistic specialists together as soon as possible so they can use their computers to create this new world language that every human will speak tomorrow.

Along with mother tongues and regional dialects (still necessary to preserve the richness of regional cultures), the new language must be taught in the schools as a first language to all the world's children.

At the same time, national anthems would be abolished. A huge competition, open to all artists in the world, could be held to compose a world anthem, which would be played at all public

90

events until planetary consciousness becomes solidly established in everyone's mind.

The same approach could be used for flags, with national flags abolished and a planet-wide competition held to find the best design for a world flag – the flag of humanity. This world flag could be hoisted above all public buildings and events, perhaps accompanied by the regional flag.

THE POPULARIZATION OF SCIENTIFIC KNOWLEDGE

"A strange biped accumulating the properties of being able to reproduce without needing any males like the flea, to fertilize the female at a distance like some sea mollusks, to change sex like the xiphophorus fish, to divide itself like the earthworm, to replace missing parts like the triton, to develop out of its maternal body like the kangaroo and to hibernate like the hedgehog."

JEAN ROSTAND

Definition of the new man, *homo-biologicus:* capable of mastering biology.

Imagine if you told someone on the street that we will soon be able to create living organisms in our laboratories, and to build computers that can talk, listen, compose music and reproduce by themselves; and that we will soon be able to live indefinitely by recreating people after death through the cloning of one of their cells. The listener would think what you've been saying is completely crazy, and would also think you need a vacation!

And yet, all this is either already happening now or is on the point of happening, and many eminent and down-to-earth scientists are working full time on these projects.

So why is there such a big difference between what the man on the street believes to be possible and present scientific reality?

The man on the street lacks sufficient scientific education to understand. How is it possible in our era that religious programs have longer airtime than scientific documentaries? It's not surprising

92

that so many obscurantist and guilt-inducing cults are popping up.

Each time a religious program is aired – say on Sunday morning – a scientific documentary with an atheistic slant should have equal airtime. For example, such a program could explain that scientists are working on the creation of life in their laboratories at this moment. It could thereby rebalance the exclusivity that religion claims to have – that only an immaterial god can create life.

Similarly, every time a religiously inspired film is shown, a program with a panel of atheist-scientists should also be broadcast as a sort of ideological right-to-reply.

Education should also provide larger access time to scientific teaching, right from primary school on. We send our kids to Sunday school, but we do nothing to inspire them with all the fantastic revelations of modern biology or computer technology.

Children, whose minds are still sensitive and highly impressionable, are being subjected to systematic religious indoctrination, both directly by their parents and by specialized organizations. It's important that we protect them from this by providing as much scientific education as religious doctrine, thus reestablishing the balanced outlook in their brains that they're still too young to get by themselves.

Religious freedom for fully responsible individuals is essential, but institutionalized conditioning, be it tacit or explicit, cannot be tolerated. There is so much religious conditioning of children in ordinary schools anyway that we can understand how inappropriate religious schools are. Accordingly, they must be abolished.

How can we justify teaching children they will go to heaven if they pray hard enough when we know it takes a rocket to go to the moon? And if parents insist on teaching such things, school must provide a counterbalance. It must not only explain that we can travel to the moon, but also explain that there are many different religions on Earth, each teaching different things, and no one can say that one is superior to the others – especially since many people don't believe in any religion and are doing just fine like that.

For example, it should be explained to children that what were once thought to be "miracles" could easily be explained rationally with today's or tomorrow's science. If it's possible to impress a primitive person with something as simple as a torch, then it's just as easy to impress so-called "civilized" people with more sophisticated technology, such as laser beams and three-dimensional projections.

Every miracle described by traditional religions can and should be explained according to our present scientific understanding. It then becomes obvious that for primitive people of, say, 2,000 years ago, any visitors coming from a more advanced civilization in flying machines would be taken for "gods" arriving in "chariots of fire". Any three-dimensional projection would be taken for an "apparition"; anyone arriving from the sky in a space vehicle would be thought of as an "angel"; and the process we now call cloning – in which a dead organism can be recreated from one of its cells – would be seen as a miraculous "resurrection", etc.

This is not about preventing children from believing in something; it's about providing them with the means to choose their own beliefs by themselves. And for them to be able to choose for themselves, we must protect them from traditional – and customary – unilateral conditioning. A deep faith freely chosen is beautiful, but a totalitarian indoctrination is abhorrent.

LIBERTY AND THE RESPECT OF FREEDOM

Two thousand years ago, we dealt with those whose ideas disturbed the norm with crucifixion, and 400 years ago we burned them, but today we lock them up in a psychiatric institution. And we've given the torturer a white coat instead of hammer, stake and nails. What was done before in the name of religion and morality is now perpetrated under the guise of mental health.

Dogma has been replaced by the manipulation of science to maintain public control: We no longer coerce "Calvinists" into "forced conversions", but have "forced normalizations" instead.

As you read these lines, many of you will think about Soviet dissidents, but you needn't look so far. The distant howling of the wolf mustn't prevent you from hearing the hissing of the snake at your feet.

Today, in 1977, in so-called "democratic" countries such as France, anyone can be held in a psychiatric hospital. It's up to those thus confined to prove they're not mad – no easy task at best and impossible at worst when faced with a panel of psychiatrists who can be both judge and jury. In fact, all mayors can presently detain for examination at the local psychiatric hospital anyone they deem liable to threaten the public order in their districts.

Imagine the case of someone who, rather than threatening public order, is simply a contender for the mayor's post. He could very well find himself confined, and because the innocent victim would be incredibly outraged about the whole procedure, he would certainly be pronounced dangerous by the psychiatrists and detained for a while. This would ruin the contender's political career, not to mention the traumatic and irreversible psychological effects.

And this can happen independently of the justice system, with no need for any tribunal and without the victim having done anything wrong!

This is exactly what happened in the U.S.S.R., except that it has been developed into such a fine art that it's a daily occurrence. But the same could happen in France tomorrow, and we must take measures before it happens. Otherwise, such actions would be considered subversive, meaning that those who recommend them would be declared in need of psychiatric treatment.

How can we act before it's too late?

First, we must ensure that nobody has the right to ask that another person be committed to an institution when the latter has done nothing wrong.

Next, we must ensure that before anyone can be confined to a psychiatric hospital, there must be a public trial giving the person the means to defend his or her actions. In particular, the person must be allowed to choose a defense lawyer/psychiatrist who can demonstrate to the psychiatric tribunal that the person on trial may be eccentric, (which can be a virtue) but is not physically dangerous to society. Only physical actions that endanger other people should be prevented. No idea must ever be stifled, even on the pretext that it is morally dangerous, because such suppression would inevitably lead to a modern inquisition and dissident witch hunts.

The tribunal should be composed of one prosecuting psychiatrist, three psychiatrist-judges and possibly even a jury of eligibles – that is to say, a jury drawn from the pool of geniuses.

Just as with any other matter of law, if the patient were judged to be deserving of confinement, he could appeal the ruling and

96

request a trial by another tribunal. In the meantime, until this second hearing, he could be confined only if he had committed a reprehensible act before his first appearance in court.

Furthermore, during treatment, the lawyer could assist the patient with matters concerning therapies, general progress and an eventual request for release. This assistance would be an added guarantee against possible attempts at depersonalization. Furthermore, the support the patient would feel from having someone impartial help him get out of the establishment as soon as possible would serve as an important factor in accelerating his healing. It would also avert the problem of having the patient's release depend on the whims of a psychiatrist – with whom the patient might feel a total lack of rapport.

To depersonalize violence is desirable, but to depersonalize someone who thinks differently is a criminal act, whether it's done with prison time, chemically, surgically or by any other means.

The tendency toward intolerance of any thought different from that of the majority is extremely dangerous, and it is escalating in France, where there is a pronounced lack of respect for freedom of thought and expression.

It's very revealing that the French Federation of Athleticism (FFA) would refuse to renew the license of a champion such as Guy Drut only because he expressed novel ideas after his victory at the Olympic Games. It's fascism when an athlete is prevented from practicing his sport because he has expressed ideas – i.e., made remarks of a dissident nature – that don't conform to those of the authorities controlling that sport.

It's of concern that a national organization would use such means of repression, and this was repression of the worst kind: repression of thought. Even worse was that no one reacted; no one stood up against this repression in a country that tells the rest of the world how much it respects freedom of thought.

Such people are totally unworthy of holding their positions and should no longer wield power; and such indifference to intolerance and fascism makes accomplices of those who don't react – accomplices to the same intolerance that might one day turn on them. It starts in sports federations and ends in concentration camps.

The Normalization of Public Opinion:
A Huge Danger

The biggest threat to freedom, hanging like a shadow over our heads, is television. On the other hand, if used wisely, it can be one of the most precious tools for bringing the peoples of the world together, creating a planetary consciousness everyone will immediately be able to sense. Through television, people can be concerned with everything that happens, all around the globe. You could even describe it as a sort of humanity-wide central nervous system.

What's dangerous is that television can also be used to propagate false or distorted information, reorganized and slanted to influence people's reactions.

Given the increasing number of people touched by their information, today's true journalists should be increasingly more impartial, and they should present only basic information. Instead, style of presentation is becoming more and more subjective, with TV hosts injecting their own opinions about everything shown, thereby tainting the presented information.

It's a good thing that opinion magazines exist, and that the public can choose to read them or not, depending on individual taste and political affiliations. On the other hand, it's unacceptable that on national news channels – which are in theory supposed to be objective – we have no choice but to listen to the opinions of totally unqualified people who put a slant on every subject. Of course, they cleverly skirt around politically incorrect topics, knowing they would never get away with them. But on any other subject, whose importance might indirectly be enormous, they freely vent their own completely biased opinions and value systems. This of course upsets those who don't agree with them and strokes those who do. More serious, though, is the way it "feeds" the majority of viewers, who had never thought about the subject for themselves: From now on they will base their opinion on what "the guy on TV" told them to think!

Where public opinion becomes normalized, this problem is potentially very serious, since it can become a normalization of thought orchestrated by the state. The solution would be to ensure that television shows present only raw information, without the slightest commentary, and also see that the shows are followed by two totally impartial specialists: one showing the negative aspects of the particular topic, the other showing the positive.

Given a balanced set of information, the public could then make up its own mind without being conditioned by unilateral opinions, which are often stupid or obscurantist as well.

Thus, every piece of information would first be presented by a neutral journalist, a "prosecutor" journalist and a journalist for the defense.

We could then hope to never hear again this phrase that is more worrysome than stupid: *"What are we supposed to think about (such and such a matter)?"*

Instead, it would be replaced by a more positive phrase, such as: *"What could we think about....?"* In fact, we should never *have* to think anything, since we can think whatever we like. When we hear obligations of thought being pronounced every day on the TV or in the press, freedom of thought is in danger. And yet no one reacts. But it's about time we reacted.

100

From the moment we believe we *have to* think in a certain way, we consider those who don't think the way we think they should to be dissidents.

THE GOLDEN AGE

The increasing gap in knowledge between scientists and the everyday "man in the street" signifies that most people have no idea of the amazing wonders that will completely revolutionize our lives in the next few years.

When someone talks about life being created in a laboratory, most people laugh. They either think it's impossible, or that it will happen only after a few more centuries. And yet right now, dozens of laboratories are hard at work on the project, with the goal of achieving it within the next 10 years – meaning tomorrow.

What will our world of tomorrow be like?

Actually, things are moving so fast – and accelerating all the time – that it would be more precise to say our world of tomorrow morning, or even our world of this evening. This is what we will try to look at together, bearing in mind that any predictions will certainly be overtaken by reality.

Earth can truly become a paradise since we'll be able to control the weather. We'll be able to make it rain at will, and will therefore switch the rain on only at night so as not to disturb the population. Since work will be entirely automated, there will be no reason to live in cold and inhospitable places. There will be residential zones in countries where the weather is warm and pleasant; agricultural zones in countries where the weather is temperate; and industrial zones in countries where the weather is unpleasant.

The human life span will rapidly increase until it levels out at 130 years. A bit later, it will increase to around 700 years.

Finally, immortality will be achieved in the sense that those who choose to can be recreated after their deaths from DNA information contained in their cells. This process is known as cloning, and we are already using it for vegetables and some small animals.

The different peoples of Earth will get along perfectly because they will have the same government, the same means of production and the same language.

Entertainment will include a type of cinema that involves all five senses – meaning not only the sound and vision we're used to today, but also the senses of smell, taste and touch. This will be achieved through a device transmitting sensations directly to the brain using specific waves. In addition to audiovisual information, the strip of film will contain information concerning the other senses.

Biological robots will be produced in large quantities and every person will have several at his or her personal service.

Learning will be done chemically, and we will be able to absorb in minutes what now takes dozens of years of painful work at school.

Every disease will be eradicated thanks to new medicine based on molecular biology.

We'll be able to choose our children's personalities "a la carte" if we wish, according to our own particular tastes or the needs of society.

Every human being will be able to spend his or her time developing the "inner self" to be in harmony with infinity, of which we are all a part.

VERY IMPORTANT REMINDER

It is most important to bear in mind that all proposals made in this book are just ideas. It will be up to the geniuses themselves to propose and put into practice their own reforms aimed at making Earth a world of happiness, justice and fulfillment for all people – without prejudice as to race, religion, culture or level of intelligence – in the context of a world geniocracy placing geniuses at the service of humanity.

Attempting to dictate to geniuses what they should do would be an act contrary to geniocracy itself. The author of the ideas in this book hopes to be considered capable of participating in the Council of Creatives, whose role would be precisely that of submitting new ideas to the wise judgment of the World College of Geniocracy.

III. The Creation of a World Geniocratic Government

A Call to the Geniuses of Earth

*"You can ignore politics as much as you wish,
but it will not ignore you."*

CH. De Montalembert

Scientists, philosophers and artists from all over the world, you who have always been exploited and betrayed by political and economic powers that transformed your inventions into deadly weapons and your art into propaganda for their ideologies: It is time to unite!

Abandon the states that oppress you by forcing you to work on projects that don't interest you. Unite to found an organization that will as its first step commercialize the fruit of your research, your work and your inventions to profit no one but yourselves!

Abandon the entities that are watching you, spying on you and checking on you, waiting to transform your equations into destructive weapons and your calculations into apocalyptic missiles!

Come to Geneva and meet other scientists like yourselves at least once. Then, after returning temporarily to your respective countries, save up enough money to associate and create this universal center of peace, the embryonic form of the World Geniocratic Government.

Rise above national borders, politics and military divisions. Don't waste your voice on deaf ears, as the ecological groups do with their unheeded warnings. Take direct action instead and create this world government.

Many globalists and federalists make the mistake of trying to create world unity by working within the pre-existing state/nation structure. But that will not work, because these nation/states are governed by people who don't want to lose their positions as governors. Those in power have vested financial interests in having the world remain divided, and they will never give up their positions and allow change. Instead, they prefer to keep the status quo under the false pretext of "non-interference in the internal affairs of a sovereign state".

Those attempting world unity within the existing state/nation structure will never succeed because the politicians will never give up the money and prestige that comes with their positions. In fact – and this has happened already – they would prefer to orchestrate conflicts and make us think we need them on both sides of the border to "defend the country", thereby justifying their salaries in the eyes of the population (or at least by what's left of it).

We must go above their heads! Are we so naïve as to believe that people thriving from living off the present structures will collaborate to destroy the hand that feeds them? Those in power right now aren't very intelligent, but they're not stupid when it comes to their purses!

No, all this is too sordid. We must rise above all this political-economic skulduggery, and without even asking those in power, directly create a world government composed of the raw material they rely on most: the researchers and geniuses.

We must take these warmongering "nation states" by the jugular. And you, the geniuses of Earth, are their lifeblood. Be aware of your power and strength, and escape together to unite and create a structure that will at last look after the interests of humanity rather than just those of the privileged few holding the reins.

And you my fellow artists, creators of art and the outcasts of our civilization: Wake up! You were neglected only because you weren't considered economically viable. How can you tolerate such treatment any longer? Just think how many millions of young philosophers, painters, musicians and architects – plus those interested in literature, psychology or theatre – have been left to die of hunger, or forced to forget about their art and take up math or live by doing some sort of manual labor, thus depriving humanity of the fruit of their creativity.

How many Mozarts, Van Goghs, Préverts or Nietzsches died at the bottom of a mine or after spending their lives behind a production line instead of doing what they were born to do – which was to create? But it wasn't economically viable for them to create, so....

Human happiness – living in a world of color, harmony, shapes and words – isn't considered a viable proposition. Some countries allocate 50 percent of the budget to the military, yet only 0.01 percent for art and culture! No comment needed.

What sort of world is this, in which Caesar, Napoleon and Hitler can command thousands of times more money than such contemporaries as Plato, Beethoven and Le Corbusier?

$E = MC^2$ = Hiroshima.

Einstein was left crying with regret that he had not destroyed his calculations before they were used to kill millions.

Scientists have just pierced the secret of DNA by synthesizing a human gene in the United States, and they are looking forward to the possibility of creating human life in the laboratory. Meanwhile, military leaders are rubbing their hands together, looking forward to the number of soldiers they can create, or to the deadly viruses they can insert in their bombs.

That's enough! Refuse the deal, but don't do as Einstein did and quit when it was already too late! Stop your work right now, and destroy your formulas if you have to. You can always renew them later on in the World Geniocratic Government research center, where you can be sure no military interest will be able to penetrate to steal them.

Take away their toys! If we had left it up to the military, they would still be using swords and bows and arrows. But no, scientists came along and invented gunpowder. Fireworks are wonderful, but the military turned them into cannons. You invented the combustion engine and they used it to make war tanks; you invented the airplane and they made bombers with it. You invented vaccines and they made biological weapons. *That's enough! Wake up and say no!*

They are there, looking over your shoulder. You can't see them, but they're searching through your reports. They're not intelligent enough to invent, but they know how to use you. You discover the philosopher's stone for them and they put it in their sling. They give you everything: a job, a salary, a title, a medal – everything – as long as you continue to make them new toys.

That is the whole point of their national institutes of science: to keep you alive and producing. For your part, you get great satisfaction from your research and progress while innocently widening the bounds of present-day knowledge. But you don't realize they're watching *everything*. Like beady-eyed hyenas, they're waiting for a morsel of knowledge to fall from the table so they can pounce on it and use it to kill thousands of innocent people before you even have time to realize what has happened.

Abandon them! Unite and protect yourselves with the requisite guarantees so that will never happen again.

Whether you're from Moscow, New York or Beijing, you are all scientists. You have one passion, and that is knowledge and understanding. You have one goal, and that is to help humanity progress and ensure a better future. Therefore, don't let the politicians and their military guard dogs steal your work and use it for their own ends!

Never forget the words of our mentor, Einstein. "If only I had known," he said. Well, now you know!

Even if you reply that they have already taken plenty of your knowledge to accumulate enormous quantities of weapons, don't give up. You can now work on ways to render those weapons harmless, even if it means finding antidotes to your own inventions! But whatever you do, please take control of your own knowledge – and that of humanity while you're at it.

Unite within the Provisional World Geniocratic Government until the permanent one is created.

THE WORLD GENIOCRATIC GOVERNMENT: THE WORLD'S BRAIN

Humanity is like a large body, with geniuses as its neurons. Grouping all geniuses of art, science, engineering and philosophy, etc., together at the headquarters of the World Geniocratic Government will make that government the brain of humanity.

It therefore becomes important to build a very sophisticated nuclear shelter under the center, for if a world conflict were to erupt before the installation of geniocracy, the genius members of the provisional government would be protected and in a position to rebuild civilization. Otherwise, humanity would again have to undergo thousands of years of slow scientific evolution.

Plan of Action for a
World Geniocratic Government

Short-term Goals (three months to one year):

1. Installation of a permanent world center sheltering and sustaining geniuses of all kinds: scientists, inventors, philosophers and artists. This center will comprise the first World Geniocratic Government (WGG), and it will set up an association to fund itself through the commercialization of its peaceful inventions and creations.

2. Installation of a school that will identify and encourage the development of gifted children and geniuses.

3. Installation of a leisure and personal development center.

4. Creation of a WGG office in every country.

5. Publication of a newsletter for Geniocrats around the world.

6. Presentation of Geniocratic candidates in the elections of all democratic countries.

Mid-term Goals (one to three years):

1. Creation of a permanent village where residents can fulfill themselves according to the precepts in this book (or as described by the geniuses of the WGG). For example, robots and automation could be used

to reduce work to a minimum so everyone would need to work only a minimum amount of time – say a couple of weeks' labor per year – as a sort of civil service. This amount of work would be sufficient to provide everything for everybody; there would be a distributive economy, with no need for money or any military service.

2. Democratic election of the Geniocratic Party into office in at least one country that will then become the world center of the WGG.

Long-term Goals (three to seven years):

1. Suppression of all violent and deadly weapons existing on Earth, either removed voluntarily by those wielding them, or by dissuasion, or through the use of far more sophisticated absolute and non-violent weapons developed by the WGG, leading to the WGG taking the reins of world government.

2. Removal of all frontiers and the creation of a World Geniocratic Government composed of representatives from every democratically defined region.

WAYS OF FINANCING THE WORLD GENIOCRATIC GOVERNMENT

Every genius, scientist, inventor, artist, etc. wishing to found the World Geniocratic Government, and every citizen of the world wishing to contribute to its creation, should pledge 10 percent of his or her revenue to the WGG as a sort of world tax for creating this system. In exchange, those who subscribe will be able to:

- Send their children to specialized schools capable of identifying and educating the young super-gifted and the young geniuses.

- Spend holidays and leisure time in the centers of personal development.

- Live whenever they wish in one of the villages based on a distributive economy and geniocratic management.

- Receive a World Geniocratic Government passport.

- Receive the International Newsletter for Geniocrats.

Help Create the First
World Geniocratic Movement

First, contact us at www.geniocracy.org.

We need to create an organization in every country that will be able to present candidates at the next elections. You can be a pioneer of this system, the goal of which is to save humanity. And you can do so without being on the left or on the right, and by being above all party haggling and disunity. Above it all, above the fray – there resides intelligence.

We are counting on you to found the first geniocratic office of your country, or to launch the first local or regional delegation.

Do you believe geniuses should be given the chance to govern? If you do, please contact us online at geniocracy.org and let us know!

BIBLIOGRAPHY

1. "Les surdoues" (The Gifted) by Remy Chauvin, published by Laurence Pernoud Collection, Editions Stock.

2. "Art et science de la creativite" (The Art and Science of Creativity) published by the Union Generale d'Editions, collection 10/18, centre culturel de Cerisy-la-Salle.

3. "The biological time bomb" by Gordon Rattray Taylor. French publication from Editions Laffont, Collection Marabout Universite, Bibliotheque Marabout.

ADDITIONAL INFORMATION

Visit www.geniocracy.org.

Official Internet addresses of the Raelian Movement:

www.rael.org
www.raelianews.org
www.raelradio.net

To subscribe to the free science newsletter *Rael Science*, send a blank e-mail to: subscribe@rael-science.org

From the Same Author

Intelligent Design: Message from the Designers

Years ago, everybody *knew* that the earth was flat. Everybody *knew* that the sun revolved around the earth. Today, everybody *knows* that life on earth is either the result of random evolution or the work of a supernatural God. Or is it?

In "Message from the Designers", Rael presents us with a third option: that all life on earth was created by advanced scientists from another world. During a UFO encounter in 1973, he was given the first of a series of messages, face to face, by one of these designers. Those messages now lie within the pages of this book - an astonishing revelation for mankind.

Yes To Human Cloning

Today's new cloning technology is the first step in the quest for immortality or eternal life. What past religions used to promise only after death in a mythical paradise will soon be a scientific reality here on Earth – this is Rael's challenging conclusion in an incisive and wide-ranging review of how science is about to revolutionize all our lives. With rare vision, Rael sketches details of an amazing future in

119

which our nascent technology will revolutionize and transform the world. Nanotechnology will make agriculture and heavy industry redundant; super-artificial intelligence will quickly outstrip human intelligence – and eternal life will be possible in a computer without the need for any biological body!

These developments are not 22nd-century science fiction. All this will happen in the next 20 years – and this book's purpose is to prepare us for an unimaginably beautiful world turned into a paradise, where nobody will ever need to work again!

THE MAITREYA: EXTRACTS FROM HIS TEACHINGS

Rael, the predicted "Maitreya from the West", shares his teachings and insights in this wonderful book of extracts taken from the many Raelian seminars at which he has taught over the past 30 years. A multitude of topics are covered in this book, including love, happiness, serenity, spirituality, contemplation, the myth of perfection, non-violence, science, loving relationships and much more. This is essential reading for anyone interested in developing his or her potential and wishing to live a more fulfilling and joyful life.

SENSUAL MEDITATION

In this book, Rael shows us how to open our minds to the future and realize our true potential. He teaches us to awaken our bodies to the pleasure of all our senses by helping us enjoy sounds, colors, tastes, perfumes and touch more intensely; and also helps us develop the ability to question and remove the contradictions, hypocrisies, taboos and mind-numbing illusions of our culture. This gift of sensual meditation from the Elohim to humanity allows us to achieve harmony with the infinite nature of all things, to enjoy the ecstasy of being, and to experience the cosmic orgasm of consciousness.

Sensual Meditation – Audio CDs

The six guided meditations from the book *Sensual Meditation* are available in a set of three CDs.

The above books and CDs can be ordered directly from: www.rael.org

SEMINARS AND CONTACTS

If you would like to participate in the festivals and seminars given by Rael in your area, please contact the Raelian Movement of your continent or check out www.rael.org for the most up-to-date list of addresses, email addresses, further details and online applications.

AFRICA
05 BP 1444, Abidjan 05
Cote d'Ivoire, Africa
Tel: (+225) 07 82 83 00
Email: africa@rael.org

AMERICAS
P.O.BOX 570935
Topaz Station
Las Vegas, NV 89108, USA
Tel: (+1) 888 RAELIAN
Tel: (+1) 888 723 5426
Email: usa@rael.org
Email: canada@rael.org

ASIA
Tokyo-To, Shibuya-Ku
Shibuya 2-12-12
Miki Biru 401, Japan 150-0002
Tel: (+81) 3 3498 0098
Fax: (+81) 3 3486 9354
Email: asia@rael.org

EUROPE
7 Leonard Street
London, England, UK
Tel: +33 (0)6 16 45 42 85
Email: europe@rael.org

OCEANIA
G.P.O. Box 2397
Sydney, NSW 2001
Australia
Tel: +61(0)419 966 196
Tel: +61(0)409 376 544
Email: oceania@rael.org

U.K
BCM Minstrel
London WC1N 3XX
England, UK
Tel: +44(0)7749618243
Email: uk@rael.org

INDEX

Printed in Great Britain
by Amazon